MILITARY HAPKIDO

POLICE TACTICAL TRAINING

VOLUME ONE

BY
GRAND MASTER GUS MICHALIK

LEFT BLANK INTENTIONALLY

MILITARY HAPKIDO

POLICE TACTICAL TRAINING VOL. 1

Written By Grand Master Gus Michalik

Edited by Fernan Vargas

Military Hapkido International

London, Ontario Canada & Chicago Illinois USA

Copyright 2014 by Gus Michalik & Fernan Vargas

The authors and publishers of this manual accept no liability whatsoever for any injuries to persons or property resulting from applications or adoption of any of these procedures, considerations or tactics presented or implied in this text. This training manual in not designed or intended to function as a self-teaching manual of techniques. This course is to be taught by a certified instructor and the manual is only a training aid used for reference.
No part of this book may be reproduced in any form or by any means without permission, in writing from the Authors.

MILITARY HAPKIDO: POLICE TACTICAL TRAINING VOL.1

TABLE OF CONTENTS

INTRODUCTIONS — PAGE 7

CHAPTER 1: DEFENSIVE TACTICS & HANDCUFFING TECHNIQUES — PAGE 16

CHAPTER 2: BREAKING UP QUARRELS — PAGE 33

CHAPTER 3: SUBJECT REMOVAL FROM A VEHICLE — PAGE 41

CHAPTER 4: WEAPON RETENTION — PAGE 49

CHAPTER 5: KNIFE DEFENSES — PAGE 67

CHAPTER 6: HAND GUN DEFENSES — PAGE 83

CHAPTER 7: FORCE CONCEPTS — PAGE 97

CHAPTER 8: PRESSURE POINTS — PAGE 102

ADDITIONAL INFORMATION — PAGE: 109

MILITARY HAPKIDO: POLICE TACTICAL TRAINING VOL.1

DISCLAIMER

Please note that the publisher, authors or its agents of this instructional book are not responsible in any manner whatsoever for any injuries or loss of life which may occur by reading and/or following instructions herein. And these techniques should be practiced in the presence of qualified instructors.

It is essential that before following any of the activities, physical or otherwise herein described, the reader or readers should first consult his or her physician or advice on whether or not the reader or readers should embark on the physical activities described herein. Since the physical activities herein may be too sophisticated in nature, it is essential that a physician be consulted.

Author: Gus Michalik
Contributing Author & Editor: Fernan Vargas

WARNING:
THESE LESSONS ARE INTENDED FOR POLICE APPLICATIONS AND MAY RESULT IN INJURY IF NOT EXECUTED CORRECTLY. THE INDIVIDUALS INVOLVED IN THE PRODUCTION OF THIS MATERIAL AND THE DEMONSTRATION OF THEIR SKILLS, ASSUME NO RESPONSIBILITY FOR ANY INJURY OR DAMAGE RESULTING FROM THE EXECUTION OF TECHNIQUES PRESENTED.

DEDICATION

THIS BOOK IS DEDICATED TO MY SON GUS MICHALIK JR., WHO WANTS TO BECOME A POLICE OFFICER

    - GUS MICHALIK.

MILITARY HAPKIDO: POLICE TACTICAL TRAINING VOL.1

INTRODUCTION

MILITARY HAPKIDO: POLICE TACTICAL TRAINING VOL.1

ENDORSEMENTS

The following endorsements are from active officers of various police forces for the Military Hapkido Police Tactical Training Course. The course was created by the Black Arts Society and is intended for law enforcement officers, police foundation students and other security related organizations.

"I thoroughly enjoyed the Seminar. Ron, Gus and the other instructors were very impressive and enthusiastic. The techniques they teach would be useful for any law enforcement officer."
L.P. - Police Detective - Forensics Branch

"I attended an 8 hour Police Tactical Training course and found the information presented to me to be extremely relevant to my job as a police officer. The tactics and principles demonstrated to me were easy to follow and very much hands on. I would recommend this type of course to any police officer in the province, country or North America for that matter. With the proper patience and practice, these techniques will easily diminish the incidents of injury to police during the course of their duties. In addition, these techniques will provide any officer with confidence and the ability to exercise force in a fashion that will reduce public complainants and gross injury."
M.H. - Police Officer-Patrol

"This course was excellent in showing the different ways to control an aggressive person. It teaches a variety of methods which is invaluable as experience has shown that not all methods work, or can be employed, all the time. I would also highly recommend this course based on the knowledge of the instructors and the amount of time and attention spent by them with each group. Care was taken to show variations of methods and to ensure that students were using the demonstrated methods effectively. I would definitely take a follow up course if offered."
Special Constable M.M., Court Security Officer

MILITARY HAPKIDO: POLICE TACTICAL TRAINING VOL.1

ENDORSEMENTS

" I HAVE BEEN INVOLVED IN MARTIAL ARTS FOR OVER 12 YEARS AND BY FAR, THE COURSE OFFERED BY GUS MICHALIK ARE DEAD ON IN RELATION TO THE PRACTICAL APPLICATION OF SELF-DEFENSE. THE INSTRUCTORS ARE VERY KNOWLEDGEABLE ABOUT THE SYSTEM OF DELIVERY AND THE EFFECTS IT HAS ON THE UNKNOWING RECIPIENT. YOUR CONFIDENCE LEVEL WILL RISE WHEN HAVING TO DEAL WITH VIOLENT SITUATIONS AFTER ATTENDING THE COURSES OFFERED BY THE BLACK ARTS SOCIETY."
Special Constable M.B., Court Security Officer

"By far the easiest form of self defense and use of force I have come to learn. It makes your subject compliant using as little effort and force as possible. Definitely a welcomed learning tool that should be instructed to all law enforcement officials."
P.W. Police officer - Patrol

"The training we received was excellent, and I am still talking about it. It gave me more confidence to do my job and put a whole new view on how to approach and handle different situations. I strongly recommend it for other law enforcement officers. Thank you for introducing me to the methods."
Special Constable J.C., Court Security Officer

I had the opportunity to experience the compliance techniques utilizing pressure point activation. The techniques we experienced were well received by all members in attendance. We were also given the opportunity to try them on our work mates, and many commented on the effectiveness and efficiency of the techniques. I personally walked away with a greater understanding of the human body and how it works, through pressure point activation. I'm still amazed at how, when simple control techniques are used, we can gain almost complete compliance without leaving lasting pain or permanent injury to member(s) of our community, thereby eliminating complaints against our members.
M.W. Detective - Professional Standards Branch

MILITARY HAPKIDO: POLICE TACTICAL TRAINING VOL.1

WHAT IS HAPKIDO

Hapkido is a dynamic and also eclectic Korean martial art. It is a form of self-defense that employs joint locks, techniques of other martial arts, as well as kicks, punches, and other striking attacks. There is also the use of weapons. Hapkido contains both long and close range fighting techniques, utilizing jumping kicks and percussive hand strikes at longer ranges and pressure point strikes, joint locks, or throws at closer fighting distances. Hapkido emphasizes circular motion, non-resisting movements, and control of the opponent. Practitioners seek to gain advantage through footwork and body positioning to incorporate the use of leverage, avoiding the use of strength against strength. The art copied from Daitō-ryū Aiki-jūjutsu or a closely related jujutsu system taught by Choi Yong-Sool who returned to Korea after World War II, having lived in Japan for 30 years. This system was later combined with kicking and striking techniques of indigenous and contemporary arts such as taekkyeon and tang soo do. Its history is obscured by the historical animosity between the Korean and Japanese people following the Second World War. Hap means "coordinated" or "joining"; ki describes internal energy, spirit, strength, or power; and do means "way" or "art", yielding a literal translation of "joining-energy-way". It is most often translated as "the way of coordinating energy", "the way of coordinated power" or "the way of harmony". Hapkido is considered one of the most effective and practical martial arts in the world. It is taught to military personnel, police forces, special forces, security units and bodyguards worldwide

MILITARY HAPKIDO: POLICE TACTICAL TRAINING VOL.1

WHAT IS MILITARY HAPKIDO?

Military Hapkido or Kuk Bang Hapkido as it is known in Korean was developed in Canada by Grand Master Gus Michalik of London, Ontario. The system has been recognized through the World Ki-do Federation and the Korean Government through the martial arts federation known as Han Min Jok Hapkido Association. Military Hapkido is not an orthodox form of Hapkido. Kuk Bang Hapkido is a modern style of Hapkido which liberally incorporates elements of other combat systems.

Military Hapkido combines the best of many Martial Arts streaming mainly from Hapkido, Kenpo and Jiu-Jitsu. The system was designed as a straight forward self defense system utilizing simple movements in combination with pressure point manipulation to achieve effective and sometimes devastating results. There are no patterns or predefined defenses. This style is strictly self defense oriented and does not lend itself to sport or competition. Due to this nature anyone can learn Black Arts Military Unarmed Combat and achieve a reasonable level of effectiveness quite quickly.

MILITARY HAPKIDO: POLICE TACTICAL TRAINING VOL.1

WHAT IS POLICE TACTICAL TRAINING?

The Police Tactical Training System was developed by Grand Master Gus Michalik to offer Law Enforcement Officers, Special Constables and Security Personnel an enhancement to the skills they already command.

The Police Tactical Training System is broken down into two levels of knowledge and competency. The Level I Course offers the participant tactical response training that is both comprehensive and compliant with the Use of Force mandates law enforcement officers are held to. Participants will practice techniques for handcuffing, personal protection, third party intervention, subject removal from a vehicle, personal weapon retention, knife and firearm disarming.

The Level II Certification Course offers the participant a higher level of response training. More advanced techniques for handcuffing and weapon disarming are taught. The participant is also introduced to and instructed in the proper use of the extendable baton. This course teaches an easy to use method of one second pressure point fighting to gain immediate and humane control over a subject. Special strobe light training exercises help the participant develop an automatic and measured response.

Both courses provide hands-on training based on realistic and situational scenarios. PTT Level I Certification is a prerequisite for participation in the PTT Level II Certification Course.

MILITARY HAPKIDO: POLICE TACTICAL TRAINING VOL.1

ABOUT THE FOUNDER OF MILITARY HAPKIDO

GRANDMASTER MICHALIK

Grandmaster Michalik is a counter terrorism specialist and master level combatives trainer. Grand Master Michalik originally started Martial Arts in 1968. Throughout his career, he has studied Judo, Kung Fu, Tae Kwon Do, Karate, Unarmed Combat, Jeet Kune Do, Jiu Jitsu, Bojuka and Aikido. Grand Master presently holds the ranks of Brown belt in Judo, 5th Dan in Tae Kwon Do, 6th Dan in Combat Kempo, Specialist level four in Bojuka, 5th Dan in Hapkido and 5th Dan in Jiu Jitsu. He was a member of the Montcalm Secondary School Judo Team for four years and trainer of the Royal Canadian Regiment Special Service Force Unarmed Combat Team from 1990 to 1992. He also fought full contact, Tae Kwon Do for four years

HOW THE CLUB WAS STARTED

The parent organization of Military Hapkido International, the Black Arts Society was initially formed from remnants of the Canadian Forces Base, London Military Club. Grandmaster Michalik, and Warrant Officer B.J. McLean were tasked to form The Royal Canadian Regiment Unarmed Combat Team from military members of the 1st Battalion. The team originally consisted of Sergeant Jim Blackmore, Sergeant Jimmy Gardner, Corporal Steve Smith, Master Corporal Scott Guilford, Master Corporal Mike Lesic, Corporal Wendell Heron, Corporal Fraser Strachan and Grandmaster Michalik as coach.

For more information about joining Military Hapkido International and The Black Arts Military Unarmed Combat Federation direct all inquiries to:

www.MilitaryHapkido.com & www.Black-arts-society.com

Seminars and instructional video tapes can be ordered at the above addresses.

MILITARY HAPKIDO: POLICE TACTICAL TRAINING VOL.1

THE MILITARY HAPKIDO EMBLEM

The emblem itself holds a specific significance. The eagle represents the offensive side of the art, whereas the shield depicts the defensive side of the art. If the shield is penetrated then the eagle is unleashed. The dagger represents the military origin from the Special Service Force Unarmed Combat Team. The sunrays signify the multitude of styles emanating from the Military Hapkido style and the wreath represents that these styles are held together under one entity.

MILITARY HAPKIDO: POLICE TACTICAL TRAINING VOL.1

CHAPTER I
DEFENSIVE TACTICS & HANDCUFFING TECHNIQUES

MILITARY HAPKIDO: POLICE TACTICAL TRAINING VOL.1

CHAPTER ONE-LESSON ONE
TECHNIQUE ONE: SUBJECT THROWS A RIGHT HAND PUNCH OR GRAB

TECHNIQUE ONE:

1. Grasp the subject's right hand with your left hand, thumb up. Using your right hand with the thumb in a triangle position, strike the inside center area of the bicep (Heart 2).

2. Holding the subject's right hand with your left hand, move in a counterclockwise direction, going under the subject's arm.

MILITARY HAPKIDO: POLICE TACTICAL TRAINING VOL.1

3. Torque the hand with your thumb on the side of his wrist. Torque his pinky finger with your pinky finger.

4. Facing the same direction as the subject, torque on the wrist like you would torque on a throttle of a motorcycle.

5. Force the subject fully to the ground. The subject should drop with back to the ground.

MILITARY HAPKIDO: POLICE TACTICAL TRAINING VOL.1

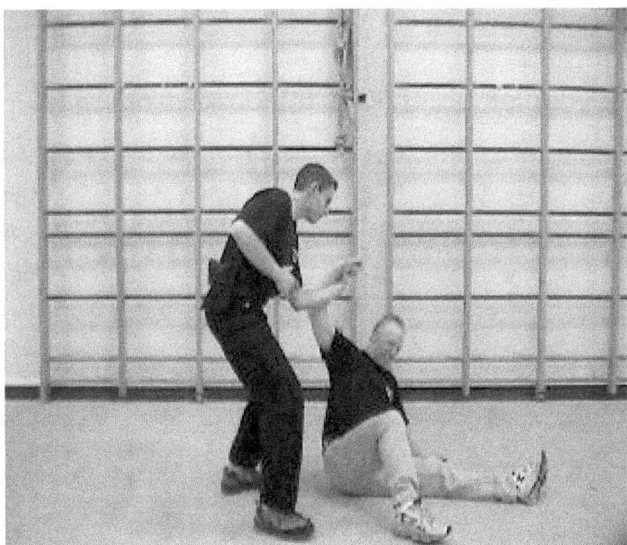

6. Turn the subject's hand downward and counterclockwise until the person rolls over. When the subject is face down, proceed with handcuffing the right hand. Torque the right wrist, instructing the subject to place the other hand towards the handcuffed hand and then continue handcuffing.

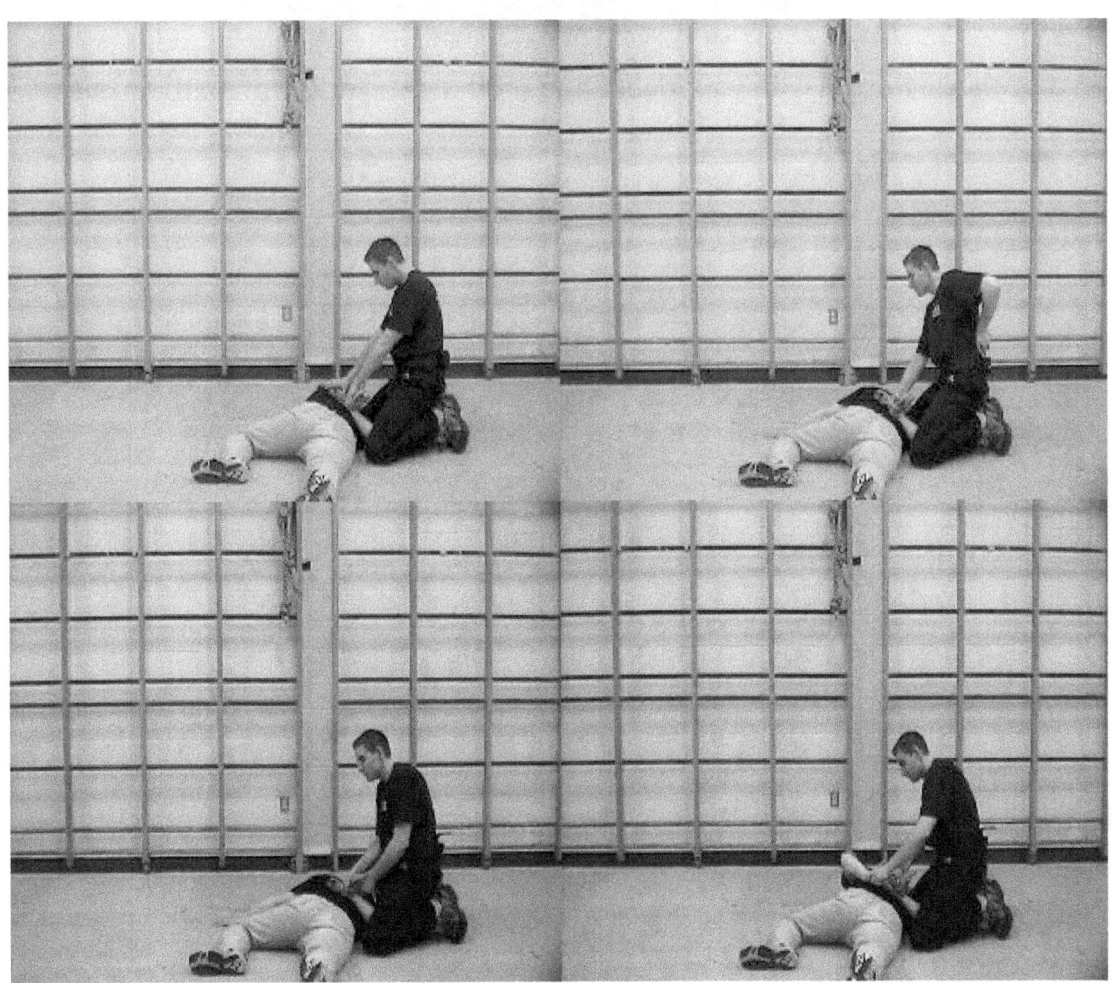

MILITARY HAPKIDO: POLICE TACTICAL TRAINING VOL.1

TECHNIQUE TWO:

1. With your left hand parry the punch from the outside.

2. In a clockwise motion with your right hand grab the subject's wrist with an overhand grasp.

3. Then strike the arm with a knife hand rotating from the bottom to the top of the back of the arm, approximately one inch above the elbow (Triple Warmer 11).

MILITARY HAPKIDO: POLICE TACTICAL TRAINING VOL.1

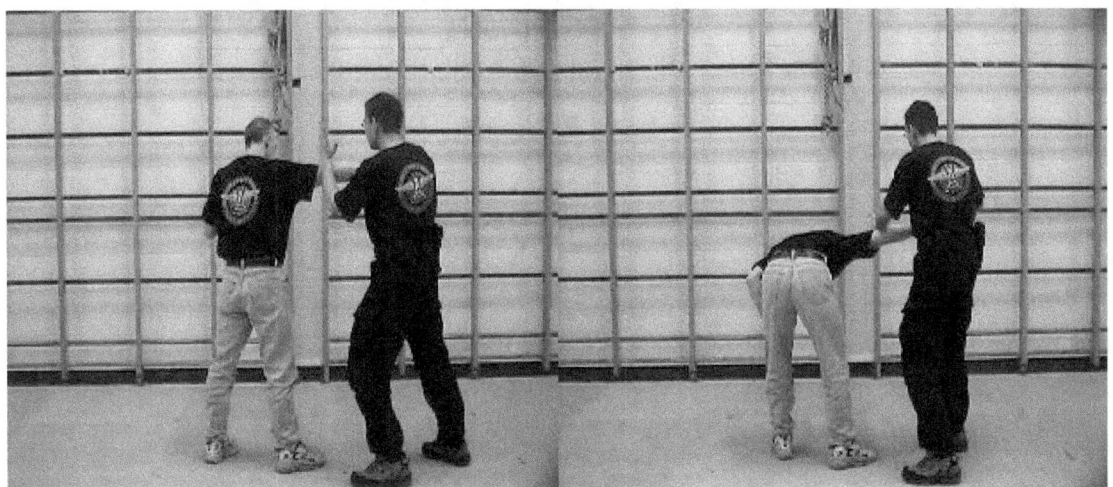

4. Place the subject's hand in an Aikido grab with your left hand, twisting the subject's arm behind the back and forcing the subject to the ground.

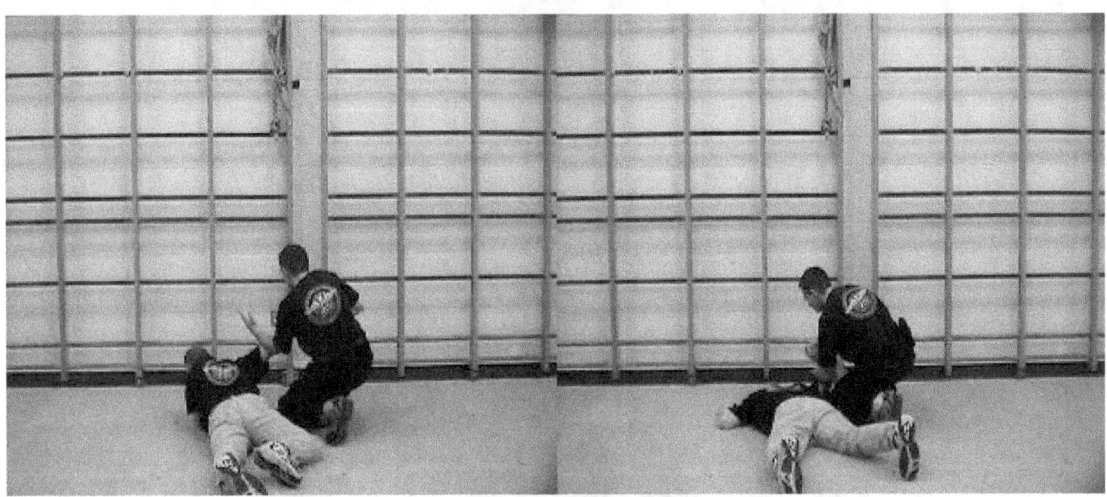

5. Using your right hand, handcuff the subject from bottom to top.

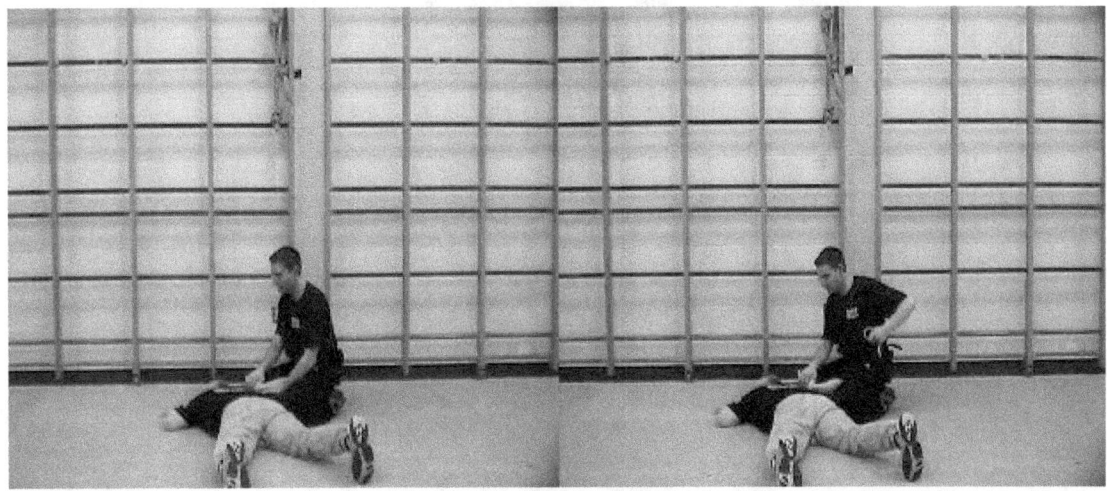

6. Torque the right wrist, instructing the subject to place the other hand towards the handcuffed hand and then continue handcuffing from the top.

MILITARY HAPKIDO: POLICE TACTICAL TRAINING VOL.1

MILITARY HAPKIDO: POLICE TACTICAL TRAINING VOL.1

CHAPTER ONE-LESSON TWO
TECHNIQUE ONE: SUBJECT ATTEMPTS TO CHOKE THE OFFICER FROM THE FRONT

1. Turn your head to the right to loosen the subject's grip and attempt to maintain airflow.

2. With your left thumb grab your subject's right pinky.

23

MILITARY HAPKIDO: POLICE TACTICAL TRAINING VOL.1

3. Turn the pinky clockwise keeping it close to your body

4. With your right hand place the subject's index finger between your thumb and index finger. Apply downward pressure on the back of the hand just past the knuckle joint.

MILITARY HAPKIDO: POLICE TACTICAL TRAINING VOL.1

5. While keeping a constant pressure on the index finger of your subject, move your body counterclockwise under the person's arm until you are both facing the same direction.

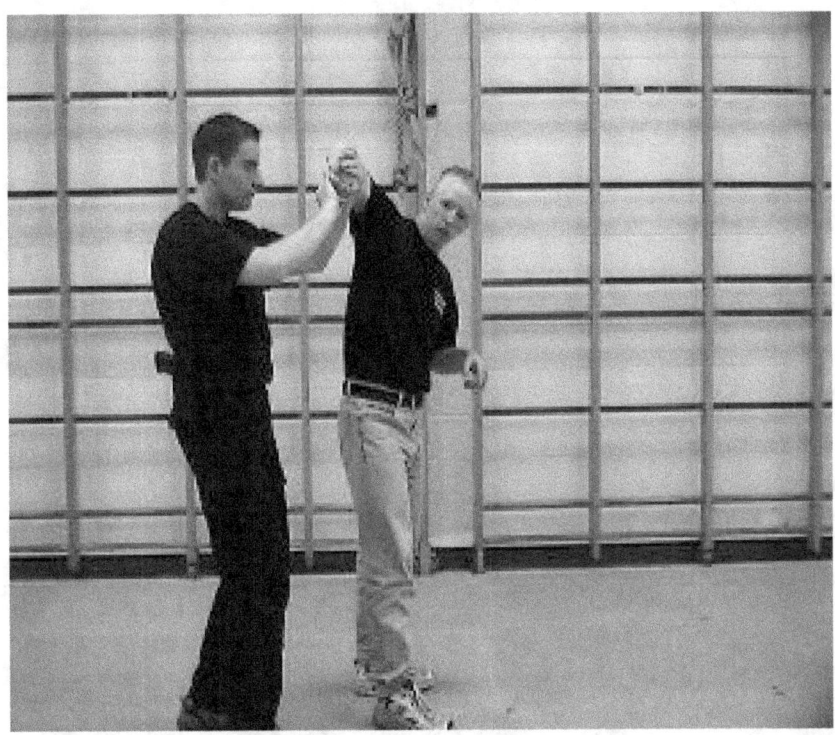

6. Using your left hand, press the extra-ordinary points on the subject's left shoulder/neck forcing the subject to the ground.

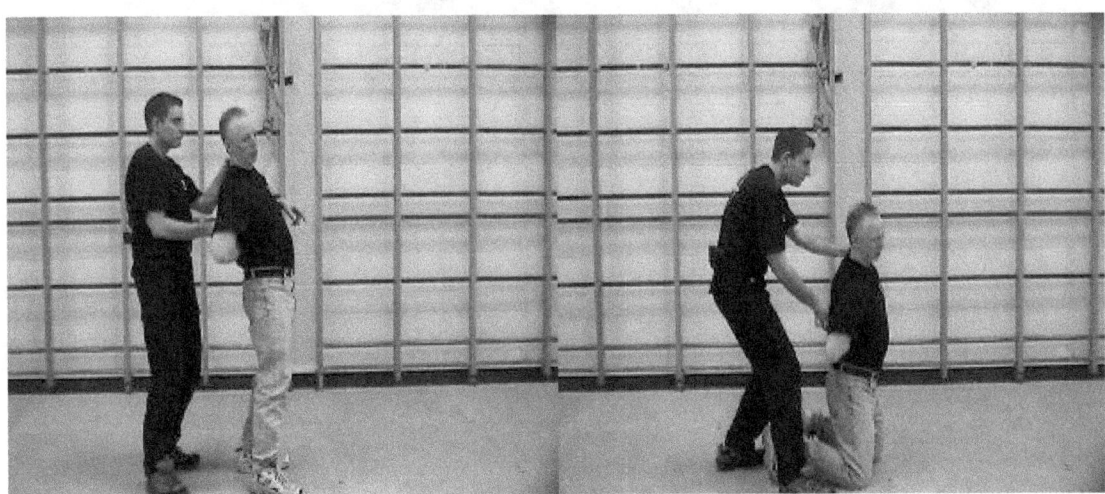

MILITARY HAPKIDO: POLICE TACTICAL TRAINING VOL.1

7. Put handcuffs on the right wrist while requesting subject to place left arm behind.

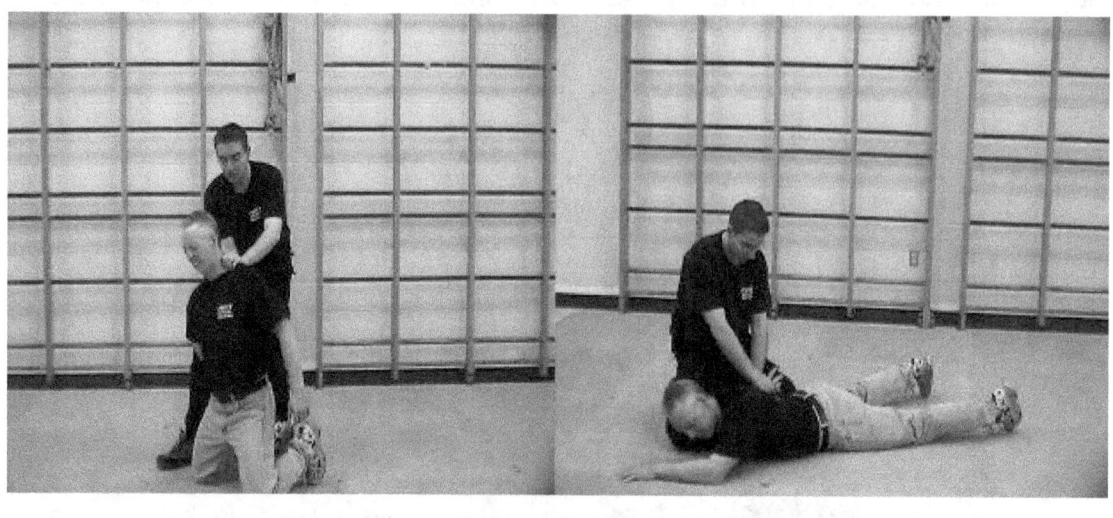

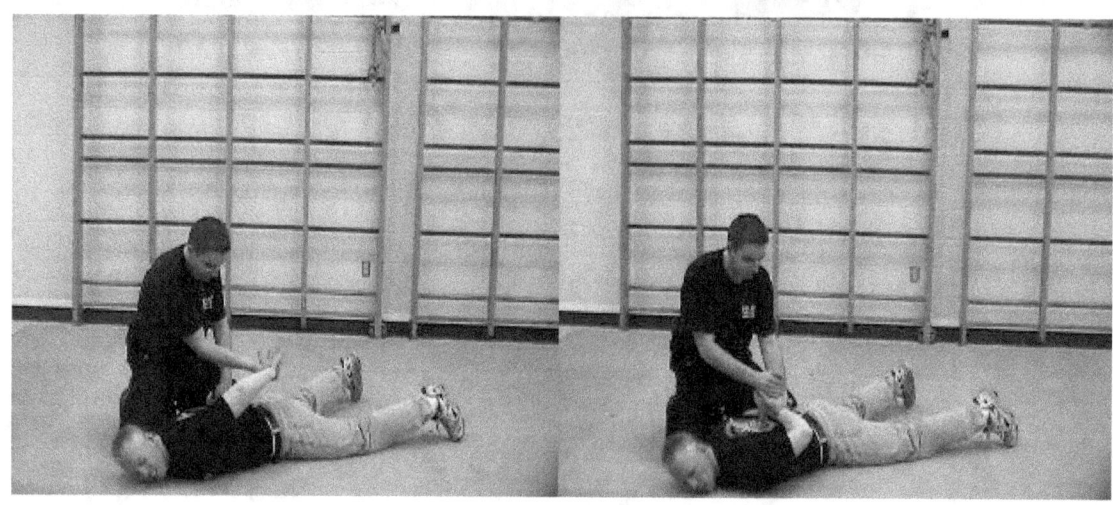

26

MILITARY HAPKIDO: POLICE TACTICAL TRAINING VOL.1

CHAPTER ONE-LESSON THREE
SUBJECT HAS BEEN BACKED TO AN OBSTACLE AND HAS TURNED TO CONFRONT THE OFFICER

1. Using your right hand with index finger in a triangle (Phoenix knuckle), apply pressure to Stomach 5 on the subject's right side of jaw, forcing the subject's head to your right all the way to the wall/obstacle and downward. Simultaneously apply pressure with your left hand to the subject's right shoulder. Your right foot should be forward, your toes pointed towards the subject's right foot. This will give the officer a strong base and be prepared to defend against a kick from the subject. <u>Option</u>: Depending on subject movement officer can initially apply pressure with the left hand to the subject's right bicep to gain control.

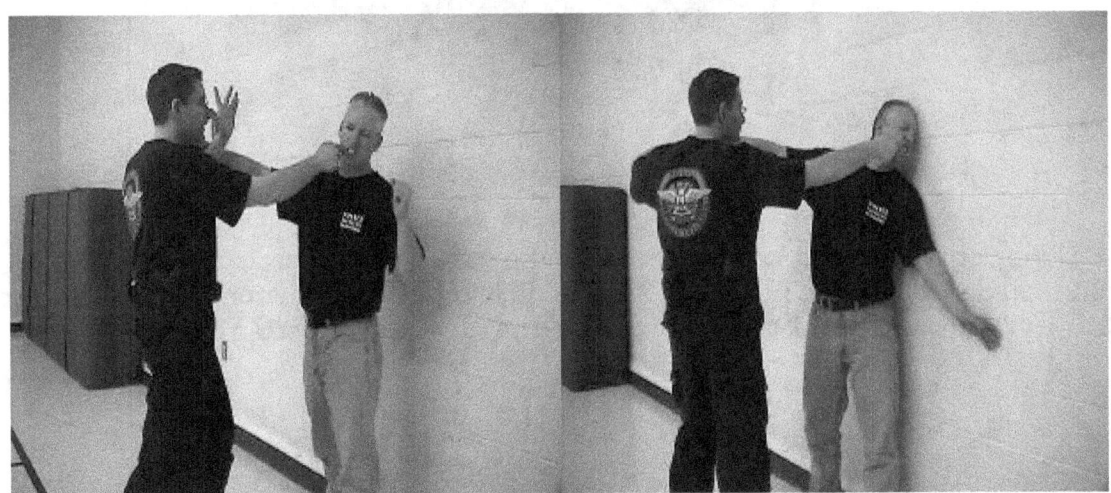

2. Slide your left hand down the subject's right arm and grasp the hand, pushing the subject's palm towards the elbow folding the hand behind the back towards the right shoulder blade. Press your chest against the elbow to form a control base.

MILITARY HAPKIDO: POLICE TACTICAL TRAINING VOL.1

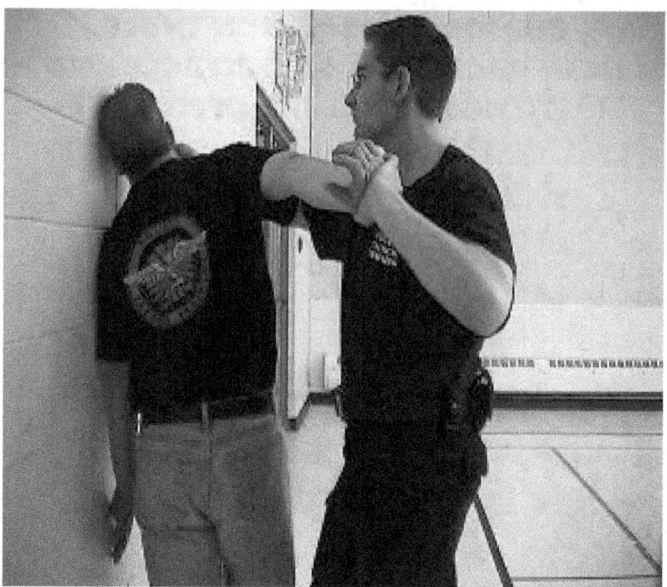

3. Using the subject's arm as leverage, spin the subject counterclockwise to face the wall.

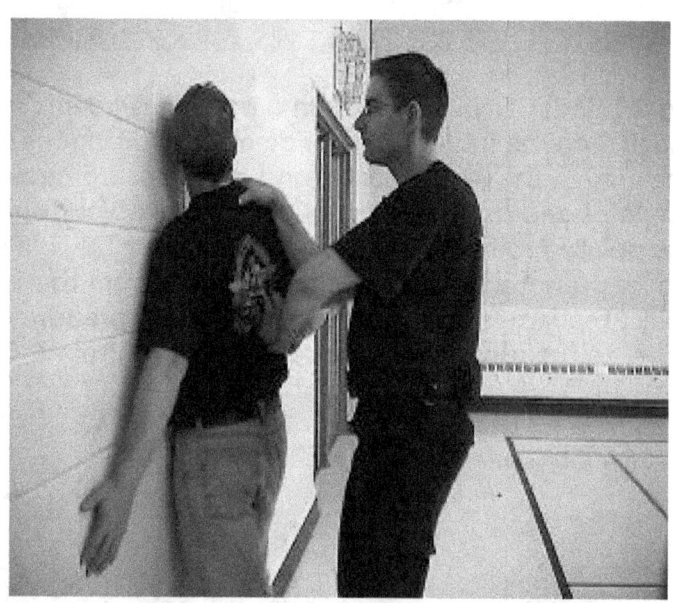

4. Using your right hand, apply pressure to the subject's extra-ordinary points on the right shoulder, forcing the subject to the ground in a kneeling position. Keep the subject against the wall and keep close to the subject to maintain control.

MILITARY HAPKIDO: POLICE TACTICAL TRAINING VOL.1

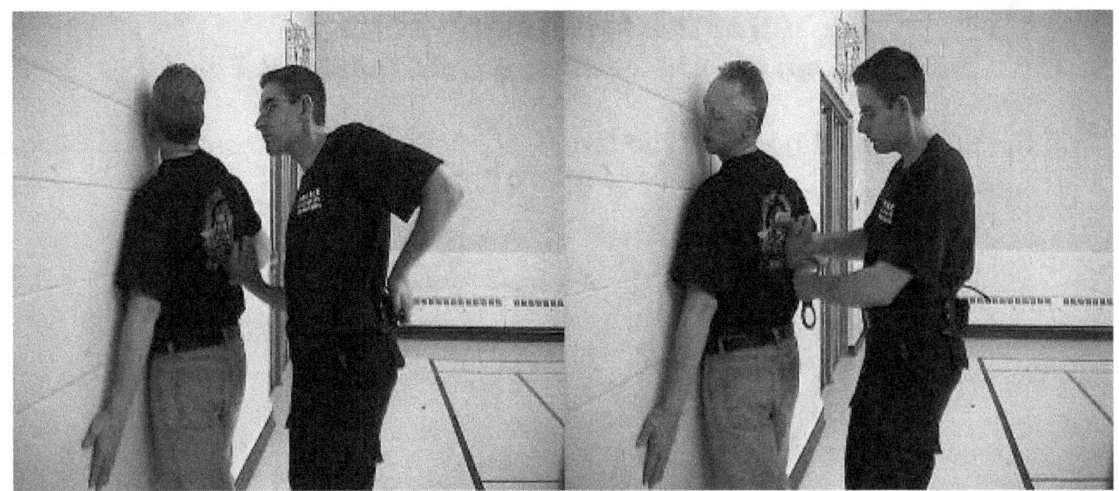

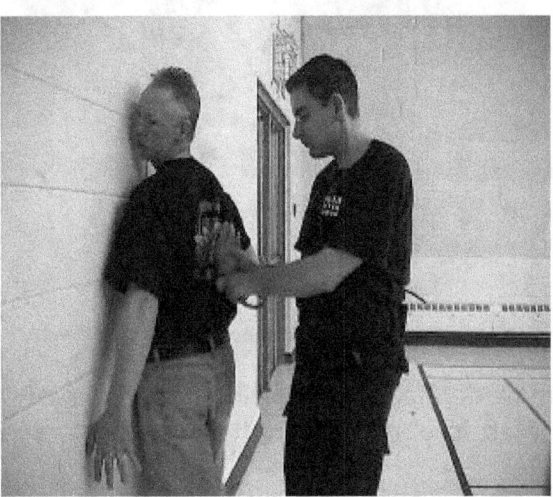

5. Place handcuff on the subject's right wrist while demanding the left arm be brought to the rear.

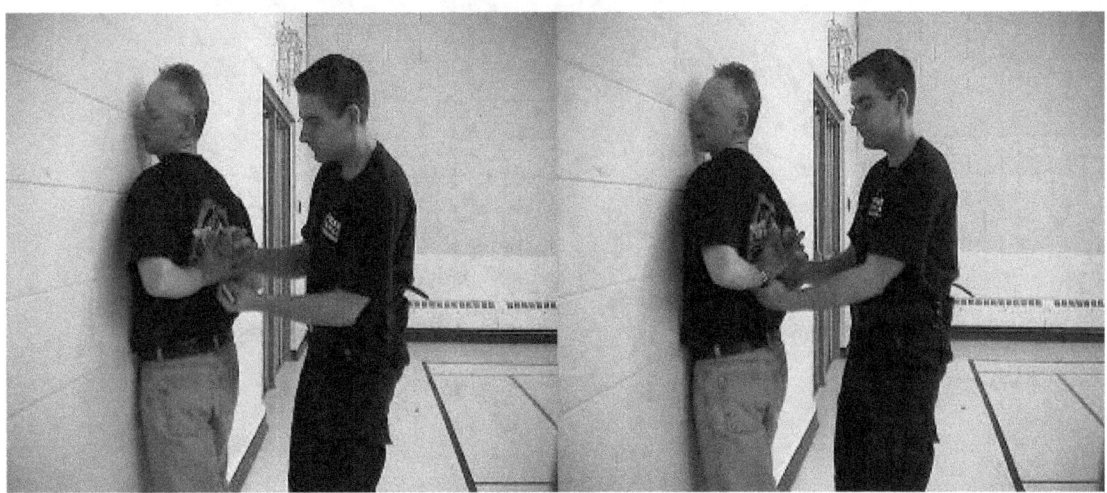

MILITARY HAPKIDO: POLICE TACTICAL TRAINING VOL.1

CHAPTER ONE-LESSON FOUR
Subject grabs the officer using a right hand lapel grab

1. Grab the subject's right hand with your right hand. Your thumb should be up using a reverse Aikido grip.

2. Simultaneously turn clockwise sharply, striking the back of the subject's arm with your left forearm, forcing the subject to release.

3. Turn counterclockwise applying a wrist lock by folding the subject's hand towards the bicep with your right forearm.

MILITARY HAPKIDO: POLICE TACTICAL TRAINING VOL.1

4. Take the subject to the ground using the wrist lock and proceed with appropriate handcuffing techniques.

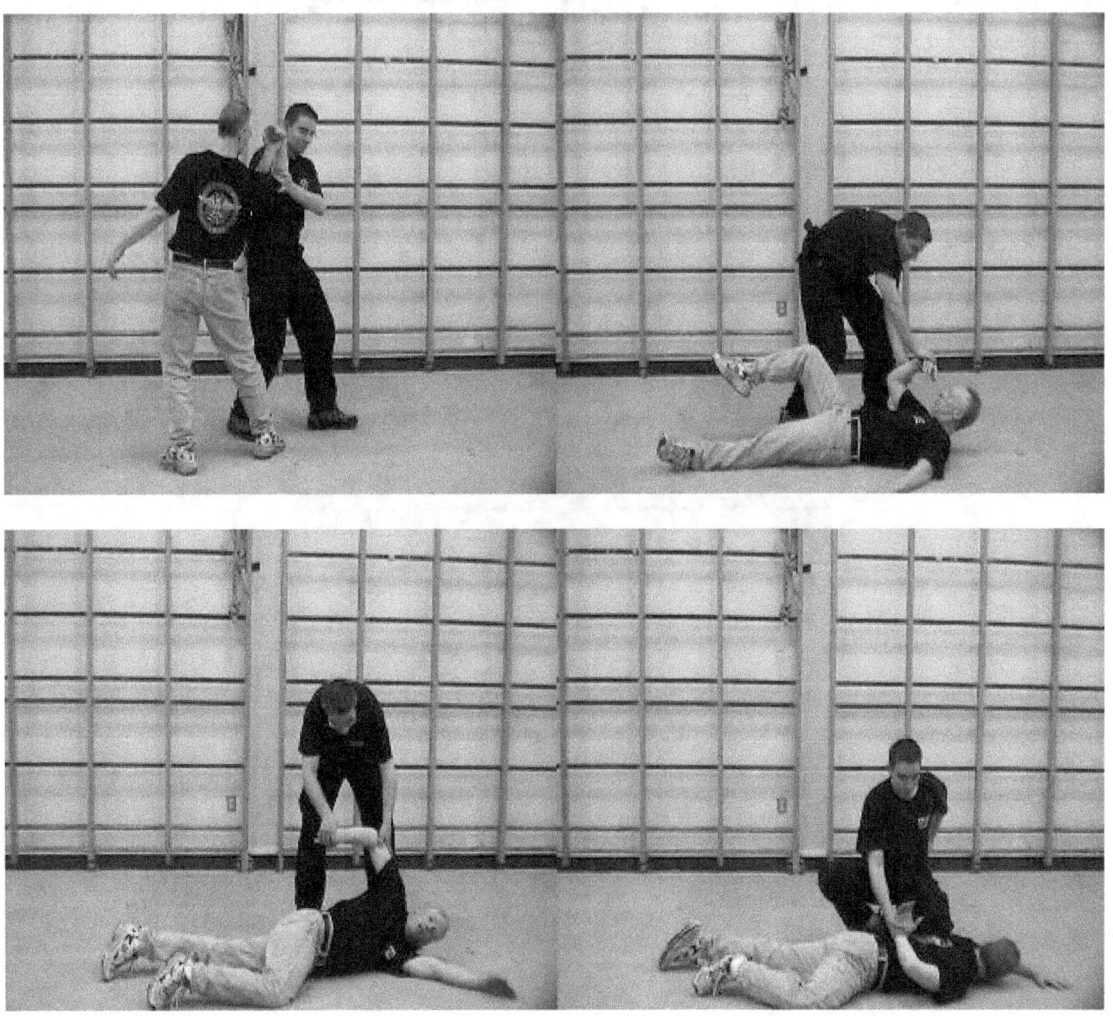

31

MILITARY HAPKIDO: POLICE TACTICAL TRAINING VOL.1

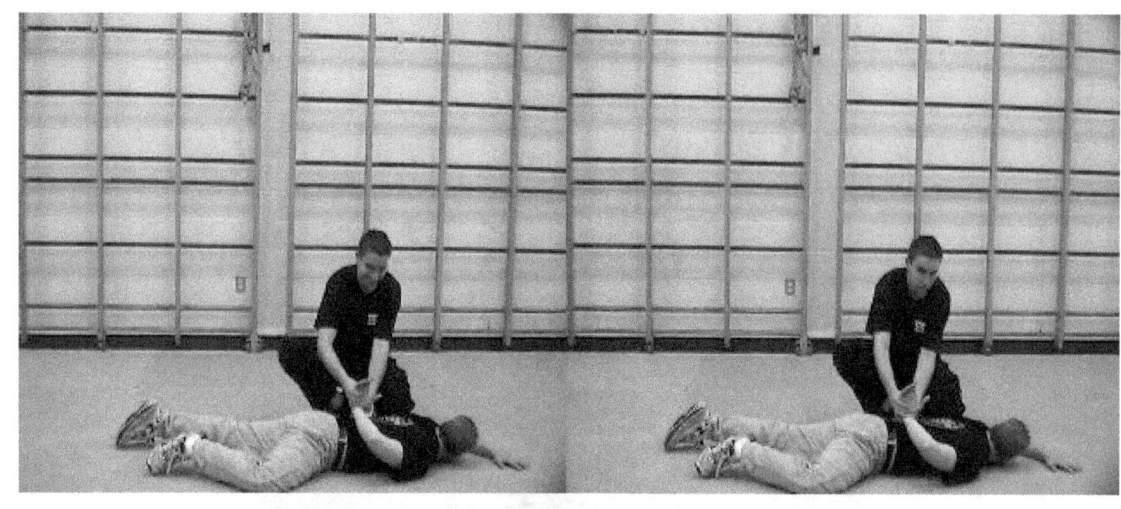

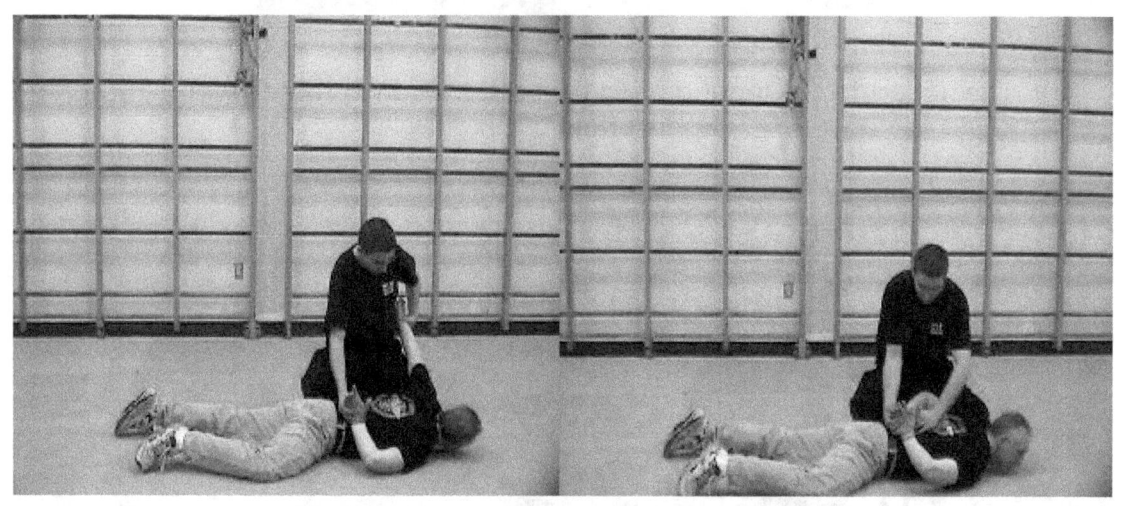

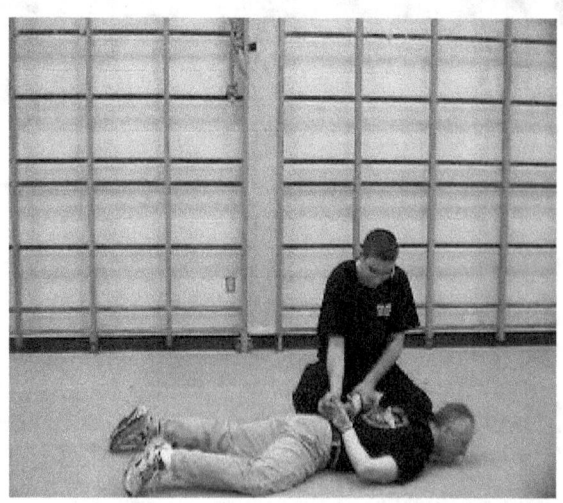

CHAPTER II
BREAKING UP QUARRELS

MILITARY HAPKIDO: POLICE TACTICAL TRAINING VOL.1

CHAPTER TWO-LESSON ONE
CONTROL TECHNIQUES USED TO SEPARATE AGGRESSIVE SUBJECTS INVOLVED IN A QUARREL OR FRAY

TECHNIQUE ONE

1. Position yourself with your strong side away from the subject and to the rear, facing the same direction.

2. Using your weak side hand apply pressure to the same side of the subject's neck (Small Intestine 17).

3. Simultaneously, using your strong side hand to control the neck, lift and peel the subject back on a 45-degree angle and take the subject all the way to the ground.

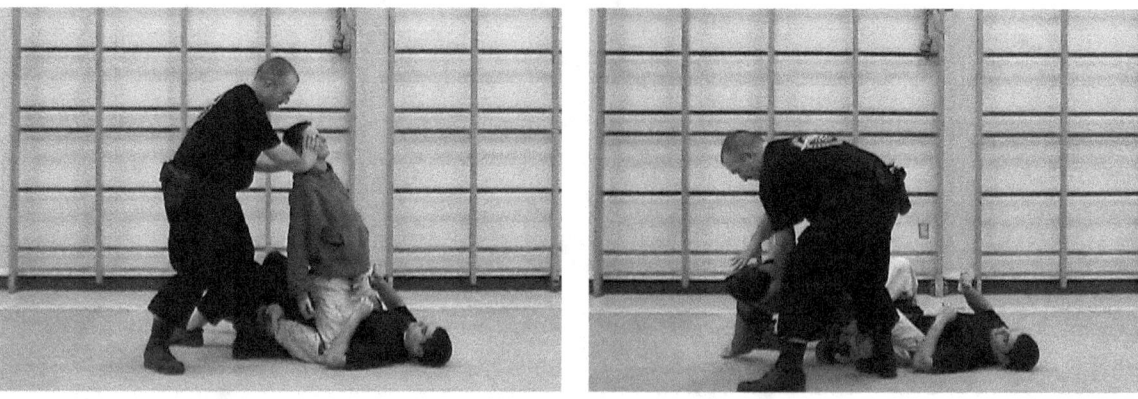

4. When the subject is face down, proceed with appropriate handcuffing techniques.

MILITARY HAPKIDO: POLICE TACTICAL TRAINING VOL.1

TECHNIQUE TWO

1. Position yourself with your strong side away from the subject and to the rear, facing the same direction.

2. Grasp both sides of the subject's neck from behind (Stomach 9) which will cause the blood pressure to lower, allowing you to peel the subject away.

3. As the subject peels away, move your strong side hand further back on the neck (Small Intestine 17) and direct the subject to the weak side and all the way to the ground.

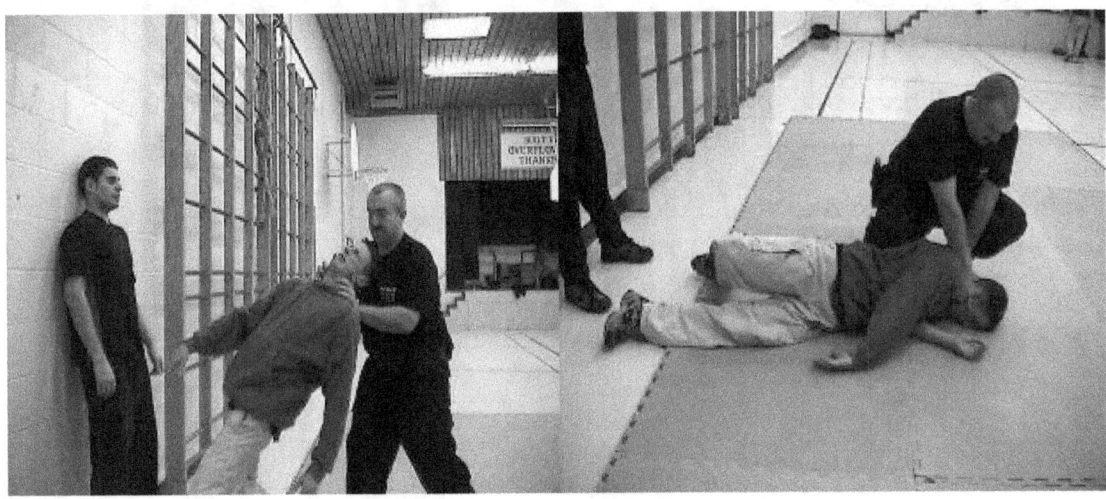

4. When the subject is face down, proceed with appropriate handcuffing techniques.
1. Position yourself with your strong side away from the subject and to the rear, facing the same direction.

TECHNIQUE THREE

MILITARY HAPKIDO: POLICE TACTICAL TRAINING VOL.1

1. Approach the subject from a 45-degree angle to the rear and apply pressure with the right hand into the bicep (Heart 2) on the subject's right arm.

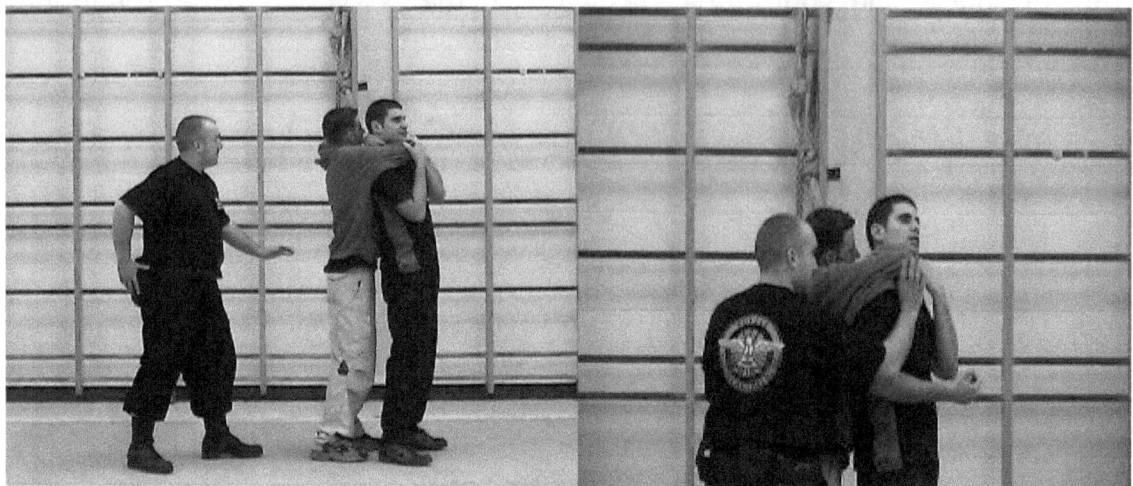

2. Simultaneously using the left hand, apply pressure into the subject's neck (Small Intestine 17) and peel the subject to the left.

3. Move the left hand from the neck (Small Intestine 17) around to the front and grasp the subject's right wrist, tying up the subject's arms.

4. Take the subject to the ground and proceed with appropriate handcuffing techniques.

MILITARY HAPKIDO: POLICE TACTICAL TRAINING VOL.1

CHAPTER TWO-LESSON TWO
CONTROL TECHNIQUES USED WHEN SUBJECT IS
NON-AGGRESSIVELY RESISTING ARREST

TECHNIQUE ONE

1. Position yourself with your strong side away from the subject and to the rear, facing the same direction.

2. Using your weak side hand, apply pressure downward on the subject's shoulder blade using your knee (Bladder 45).

3. Using your strong side hand, apply pressure to the subject's extra-ordinary point on the furthest side of the neck (HN 14).

MILITARY HAPKIDO: POLICE TACTICAL TRAINING VOL.1

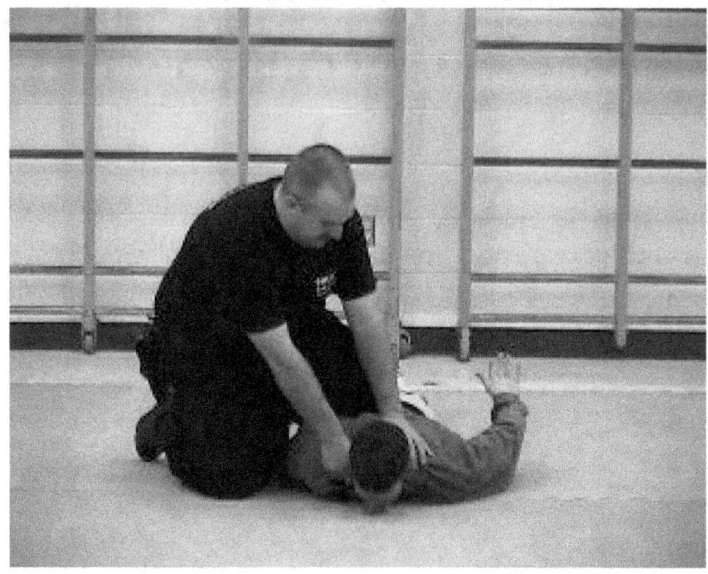

4. Demand the subject's hands to the rear and proceed with the appropriate handcuffing techniques.

MILITARY HAPKIDO: POLICE TACTICAL TRAINING VOL.1

TECHNIQUE ONE

1. Officer A takes a position with strong side away from the subject and to the rear, facing the same direction. While Officer B takes position near the subject's feet.

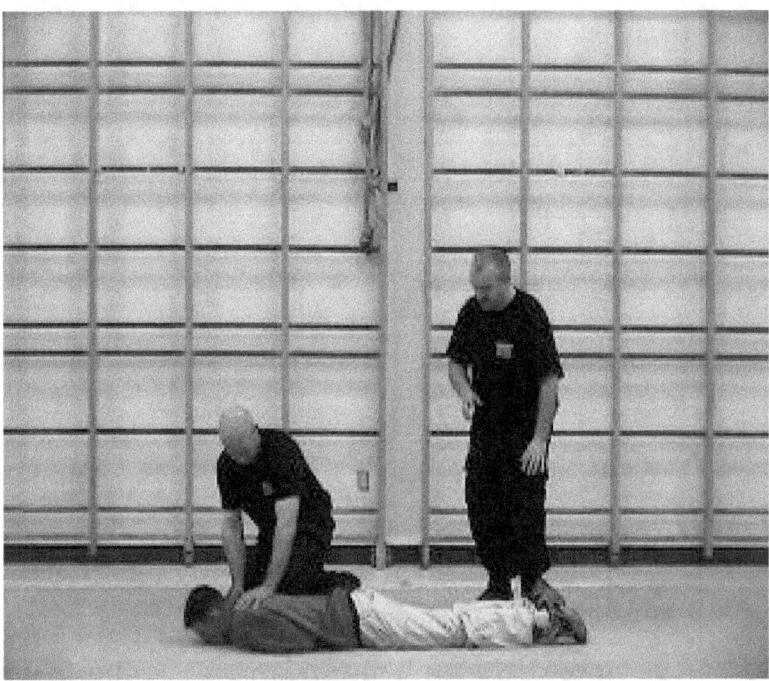

2. Officer A places hand on back of subject's opposite shoulder.

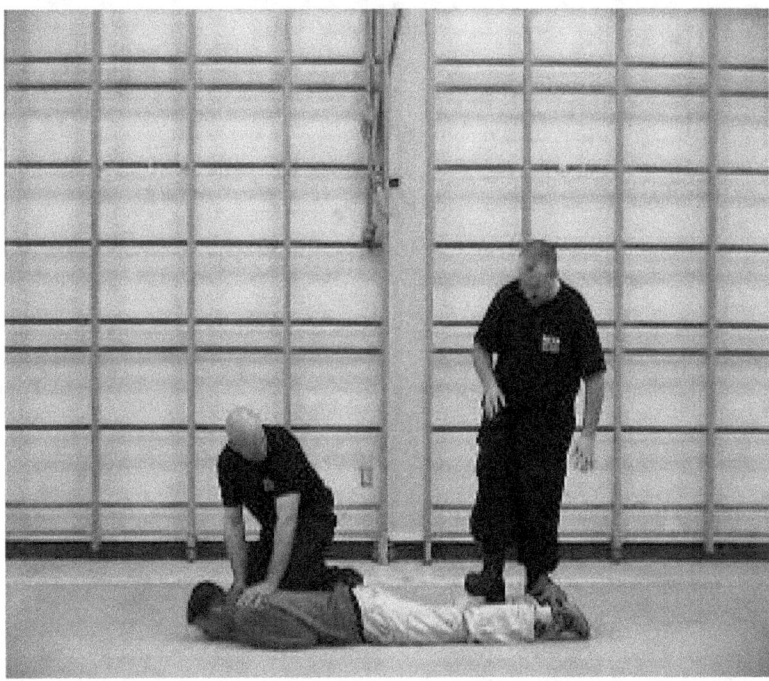

MILITARY HAPKIDO: POLICE TACTICAL TRAINING VOL.1

3. Officer B places foot against the closest leg of the subject for control while placing the heel of the other foot on the back of the closest leg at the inside base of the calf muscle (Triple Yin - Kidney 0), applying pressure to roll the subject.

4. Officer A controls the subject's upper body and applies handcuffs while Officer B continues to apply pressure to the subject's ankles.

MILITARY HAPKIDO: POLICE TACTICAL TRAINING VOL.1

CHAPTER III
SUBJECT REMOVAL FROM A VEHICLE

MILITARY HAPKIDO: POLICE TACTICAL TRAINING VOL.1

CHAPTER THREE-LESSON ONE
CONTROL TECHNIQUES TO REMOVE A SUBJECT FROM A VEHICLE

TECHNIQUE ONE

1. Approaching from the driver side with the door open, control the subject by using your right leg to block into the subject's thigh.

2. Place your left hand on the subject's left shoulder to control body movement.

MILITARY HAPKIDO: POLICE TACTICAL TRAINING VOL.1

3. Simultaneously using your right hand, reach over the top of the subject's arm and pull the thumb of the subject's left hand back in a straight line with the subject's arm causing the subject to release the steering wheel.

4. Continue the motion by turning the subject's arm downward and pulling the subject's elbow into your body to maintain control.

5. Pull the subject's arm to the rear and force the subject's hand upward.

MILITARY HAPKIDO: POLICE TACTICAL TRAINING VOL.1

6. Reach over the subject's shoulder with your left hand, attaining a wristlock while sliding the right hand down to the elbow to maintain control.

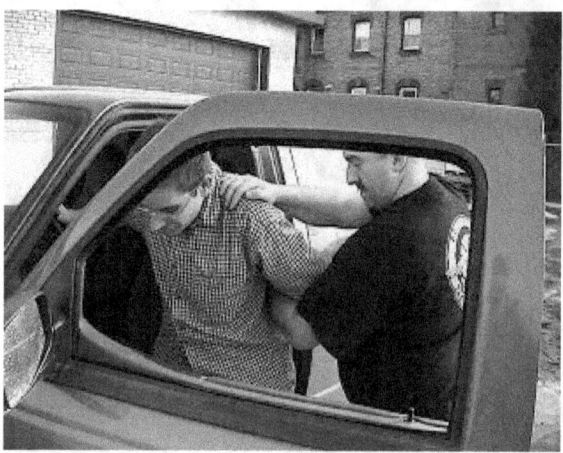

7. Maintaining control of the arm, lift the subject from the vehicle. Turning counterclockwise walk the subject to the rear of the vehicle.

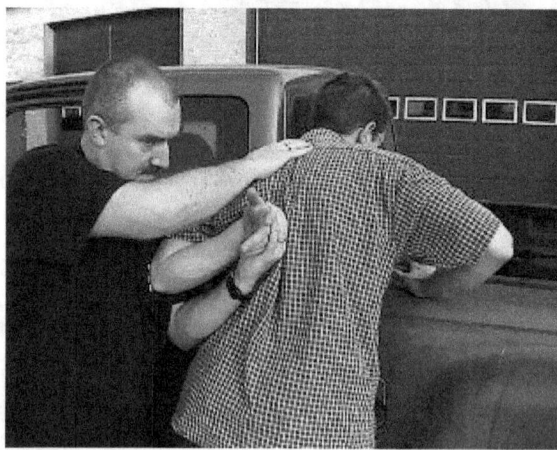

8. Proceed with appropriate handcuffing techniques.

MILITARY HAPKIDO: POLICE TACTICAL TRAINING VOL.1

TECHNIQUE TWO

1. Approaching from the driver side with the door open, control the subject by using your right leg to block into the subject's thigh.

2. Using the small knuckle of the left hand strike the subject's forearm one inch below the elbow (Large Intestine 10 & 11).

3. Simultaneously using the heel of the right hand, strike the inside of the subject's wrist (Lung 7).

MILITARY HAPKIDO: POLICE TACTICAL TRAINING VOL.1

4. As the subject releases, take an overhand grasp of the subject's left hand with your right hand and apply a wristlock. Slide your left hand under and grasp your own wrist to reinforce the wristlock.

5. Maintaining control of the arm, lift the subject from the vehicle. Turning counterclockwise walk the subject to the rear of the vehicle.

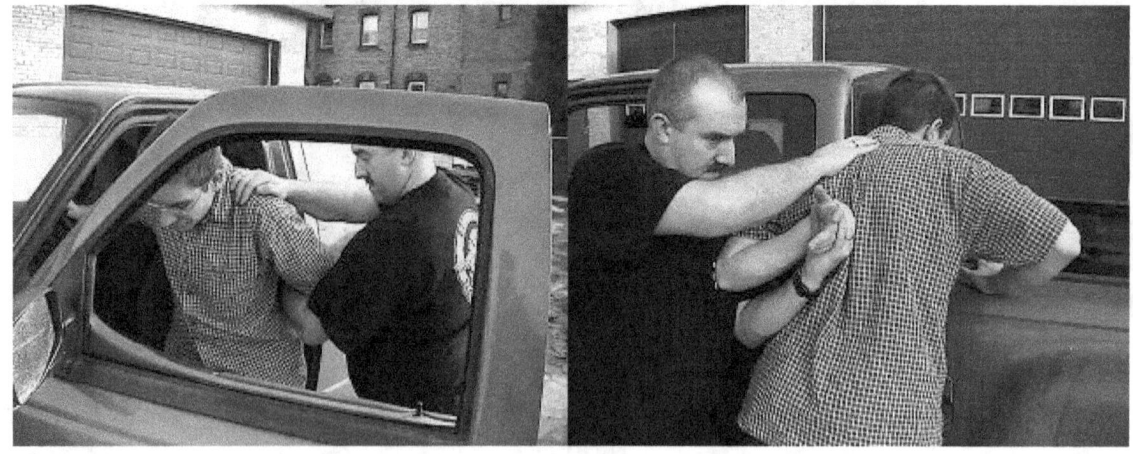

6. Proceed with appropriate handcuffing techniques.

TECHNIQUE THREE

MILITARY HAPKIDO: POLICE TACTICAL TRAINING VOL.1

1. Approaching from the driver side with the door open, control the subject by using your right leg to block into the subject's thigh.

2. Place your left hand on the subject's left shoulder to control body movement.

3. Strike the back of the subject's left hand with the knuckles of your right.

4. Continuing the motion, slide your left hand down the subject's arm to the subject's hand, torqueing downward into a wrist lock.

MILITARY HAPKIDO: POLICE TACTICAL TRAINING VOL.1

5. Feed the subject's hand downward, underneath the subject's arm into an extended arm lock. Ensure to place your small fingers across the inside of the subject's wrist while your thumbs apply pressure to the back of the hand.

6. Maintaining control of the arm, lift the subject from the vehicle. Turning counterclockwise walk the subject to the rear of the vehicle.

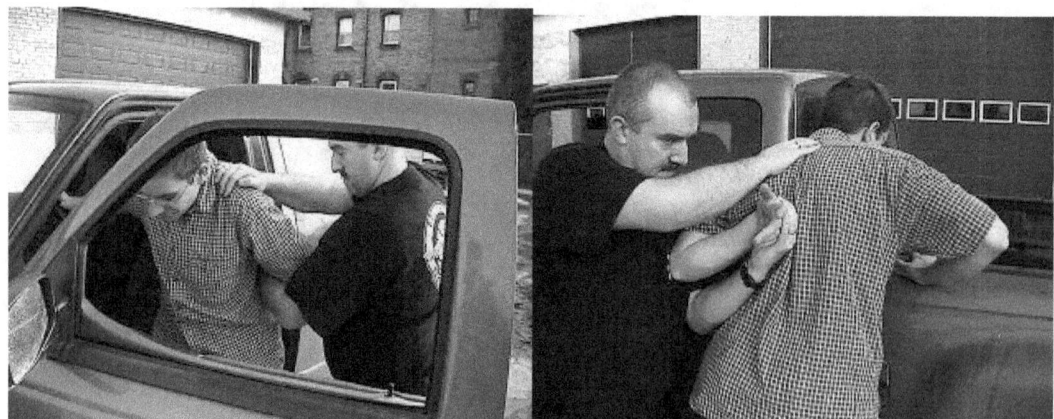

7. Proceed with appropriate handcuffing techniques.

MILITARY HAPKIDO: POLICE TACTICAL TRAINING VOL.1

CHAPTER IV
WEAPON RETENTION

MILITARY HAPKIDO: POLICE TACTICAL TRAINING VOL.1

CHAPTER FOUR-LESSON ONE
SUBJECT ATTEMPTS TO TAKE OFFICER'S SIDEARM FROM THE FRONT

TECHNIQUE ONE

1. Grab and control the holster and sidearm with your right hand.

2. Grab the subject's left wrist with your right hand and turn clockwise into the subject's arm. Simultaneously strike the crease of the subject's arm with your left hand.

3. Turning counterclockwise strike the subject's neck with your left forearm.

MILITARY HAPKIDO: POLICE TACTICAL TRAINING VOL.1

4. Continue the motion with your left arm, snaking it around the subject's head, forcing the subject's head into your armpit while forcing the chin to the side. Ensure to turn your strong side away from the subject.

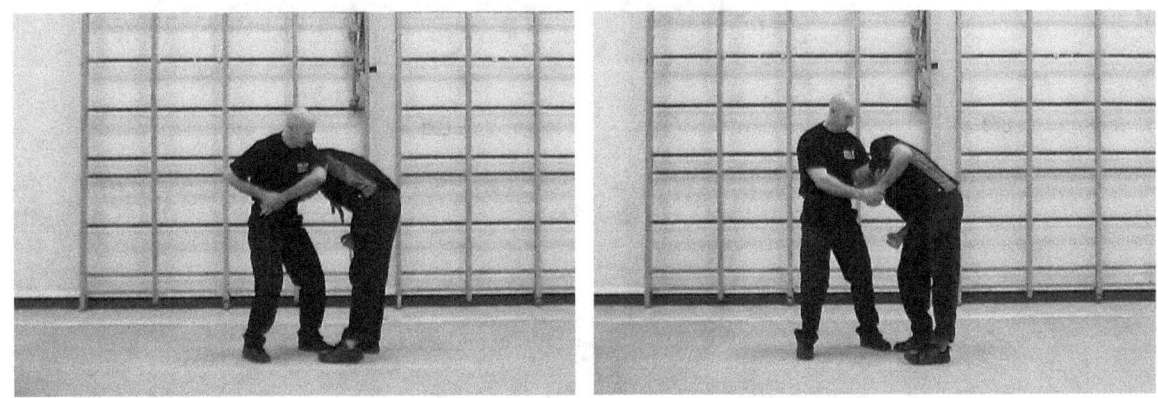

5. Strike the carotid artery with your free hand, causing a stun or knock-out.

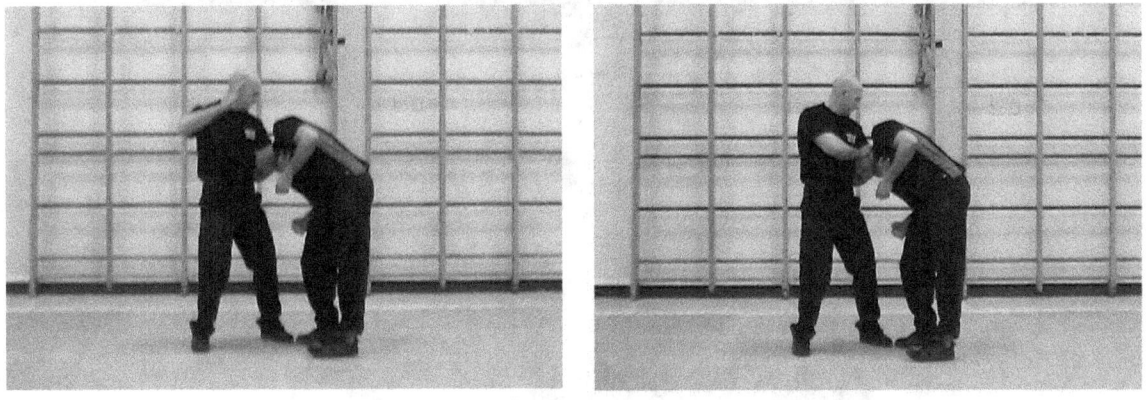

6. Perform your handcuffing drills as required.

TECHNIQUE TWO

MILITARY HAPKIDO: POLICE TACTICAL TRAINING VOL.1

1. Grab and control the holster and sidearm with your strong hand.

2. Grab the subject's left wrist with your right hand and turn clockwise into the subject's arm. Simultaneously strike the crease of the subject's arm with your left hand.

MILITARY HAPKIDO: POLICE TACTICAL TRAINING VOL.1

3. Turning counterclockwise strike the subject's neck with your left forearm.

2. 4. Continue the motion with your left arm, snaking it around the subject's head, forcing the subject's head into your armpit while forcing the chin to the side. Ensure to turn your strong side away from the subject.

MILITARY HAPKIDO: POLICE TACTICAL TRAINING VOL.1

5. Strike the carotid artery with your free hand, causing a stun or knock-out.

MILITARY HAPKIDO: POLICE TACTICAL TRAINING VOL.1

6. Perform your handcuffing drills as required.

TECHNIQUE THREE

MILITARY HAPKIDO: POLICE TACTICAL TRAINING VOL.1

1. Grab and control the holster and sidearm with your strong hand.

2. Turn clockwise sharply, overextending the subject's arm. Use your left arm and body as a leverage point.

MILITARY HAPKIDO: POLICE TACTICAL TRAINING VOL.1

3. As the subject is forced forward strike the base of the skull (Gallbladder 20) with an inside ridge-hand with your left hand. This will cause a stun or possible knock-out.

MILITARY HAPKIDO: POLICE TACTICAL TRAINING VOL.1

4. Peel the subject's right hand from the sidearm and fold the hand back into a wrist throw.

5. Perform your handcuffing drills as required.

58

MILITARY HAPKIDO: POLICE TACTICAL TRAINING VOL.1

TECHNIQUE FOUR

1. Grab and control the holster and sidearm with your strong hand.

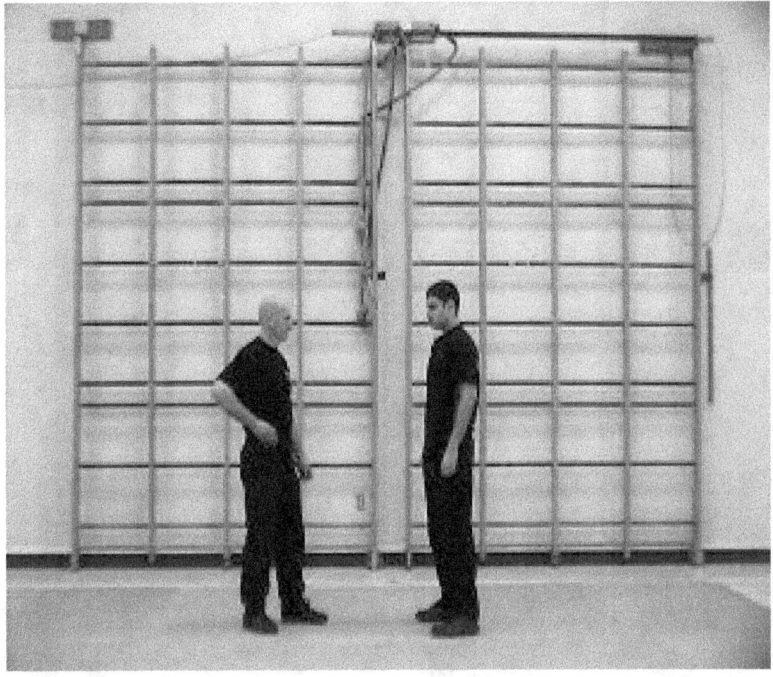

2. Turn clockwise sharply, overextending the subject's arm. Use your body as a leverage point.

MILITARY HAPKIDO: POLICE TACTICAL TRAINING VOL.1

3. As the subject is forced forward strike the base of the skull (Gallbladder 20) with an inside ridge-hand with your left hand. This will cause a stun or possible knock-out.

4. Perform your handcuffing drills as required.

MILITARY HAPKIDO: POLICE TACTICAL TRAINING VOL.1

CHAPTER FOUR-LESSON TWO
SUBJECT ATTEMPTS TO TAKE OFFICER'S SIDEARM FROM BEHIND

TECHNIQUE ONE

1. Grab and control the holster and sidearm with your right hand.

2. Turn into the subject, striking the middle of his right bicep with your left forearm.

3. Then with your left hand strike the right side of the subject's ribcage.

MILITARY HAPKIDO: POLICE TACTICAL TRAINING VOL.1

4. Then with your right hand, open-palm strike the center of the subject's forehead.

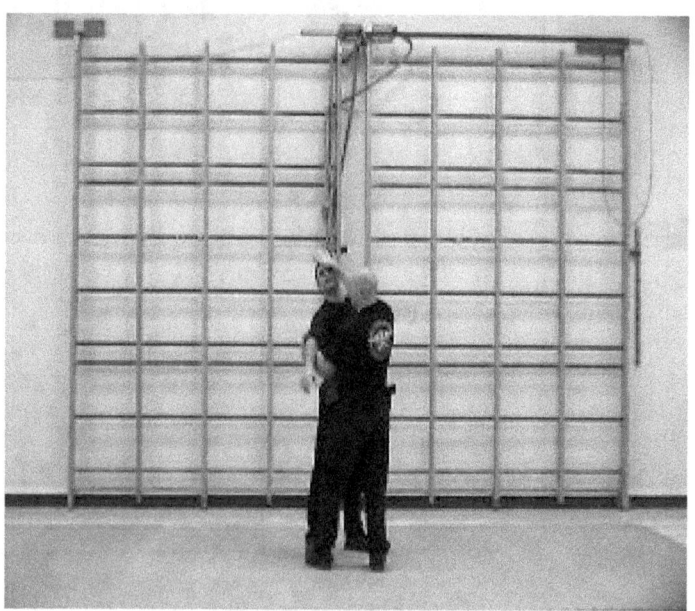

5. Proceed with appropriate handcuffing techniques.

MILITARY HAPKIDO: POLICE TACTICAL TRAINING VOL.1

TECHNIQUE 2

1. Grab and control the holster and sidearm with your right hand.

2. Turning clockwise, slide your left hand down the subject's arm and grasp the subject's hand peeling it from the sidearm.

MILITARY HAPKIDO: POLICE TACTICAL TRAINING VOL.1

3. Continue the motion, rotating the subject's arm with both hands, forcing the subject to the ground using an extended arm lock.

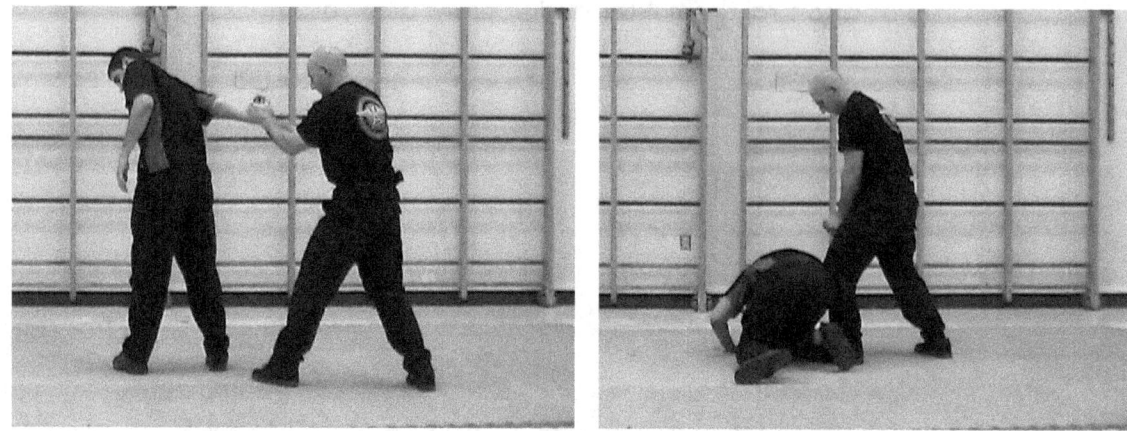

4. Proceed with appropriate handcuffing techniques.

64

MILITARY HAPKIDO: POLICE TACTICAL TRAINING VOL.1

TECHNIQUE 3

1. Grab and control the holster and sidearm with your right hand.

2. Turning counterclockwise into the subject, strike the subject's left elbow with your left forearm.

3. Continue the motion striking the base of the skull upward on a 45-degree angle (Gallbladder 20), causing a stun or possible knock-out.

MILITARY HAPKIDO: POLICE TACTICAL TRAINING VOL.1

4. Proceed with appropriate handcuffing techniques.

MILITARY HAPKIDO: POLICE TACTICAL TRAINING VOL.1

CHAPTER V
KNIFE DEFENSE

MILITARY HAPKIDO: POLICE TACTICAL TRAINING VOL.1

CHAPTER FIVE=LESSON ONE
DEFENSE AGAINST A LEFT SIDE OF THE NECK SABER SLASH

1. With an up and down block, move into the inside of the subject, simultaneously blocking the strike.

2. With your right hand strike his 3rd rib or LV-14 (quadrant 1) with the back of your hand.

3. Continue the back hand movement from left to right, then thrust forward with a reverse ridge hand into LI-18 (quadrant 2).

4. Proceed with appropriate handcuffing techniques.

MILITARY HAPKIDO: POLICE TACTICAL TRAINING VOL.1

CHAPTER FIVE-LESSON TWO
DEFENSE AGAINST A REVERSE FEMORAL ARTERY SLASH

1. Lower block with the back of your left arm from the outside of the subject's body as you strike GB-1 (temple, quadrant 1) with a downward strike.

2. Proceed with appropriate handcuffing techniques.

MILITARY HAPKIDO: POLICE TACTICAL TRAINING VOL.1

CHAPTER FIVE-LESSON THREE
DEFENSE AGAINST A FORWARD FEMORAL ARTERY SLASH

1. From the inside of the subject's body strike with the back of your right arm with an up and down block to PC-6,7.

2. Go to the right side of his body (quadrant 1) striking the neck from SI-16 to ST-5 then reverse your grip on the back of his neck from palm out to palm in digging into the subject's neck (GB-20, quadrant 2).

MILITARY HAPKIDO: POLICE TACTICAL TRAINING VOL.1

3. Continue the circular motion, shooting your right arm along the subject's jaw forcing the head to the side and into your armpit while lifting.

4. Apply pressure to LI-17 on the subject's jaw to help maintain control.

5. Take the subject to the ground under control and proceed with appropriate handcuffing techniques.

MILITARY HAPKIDO: POLICE TACTICAL TRAINING VOL.1

CHAPTER FIVE-LESSON FOUR
DEFENSE AGAINST A HIGH BACKSLASH TO THE SIDE OF THE NECK

1. From the outside of the body with a reverse up and down block, strike the back of the subject's arm.

2. Reverse the up and down block with the left hand striking TW-11 and rolling the back of the arm.

3. Take the subject to the ground under control and proceed with appropriate handcuffing techniques.

MILITARY HAPKIDO: POLICE TACTICAL TRAINING VOL.1

CHAPTER FIVE-LESSON FIVE
DEFENSE AGAINST A STRIKE TO THE HEART
WITH A STRAIGHT SABER SLASH

1. From the outside of the subject, strike LI-10, 11 with your left hand.

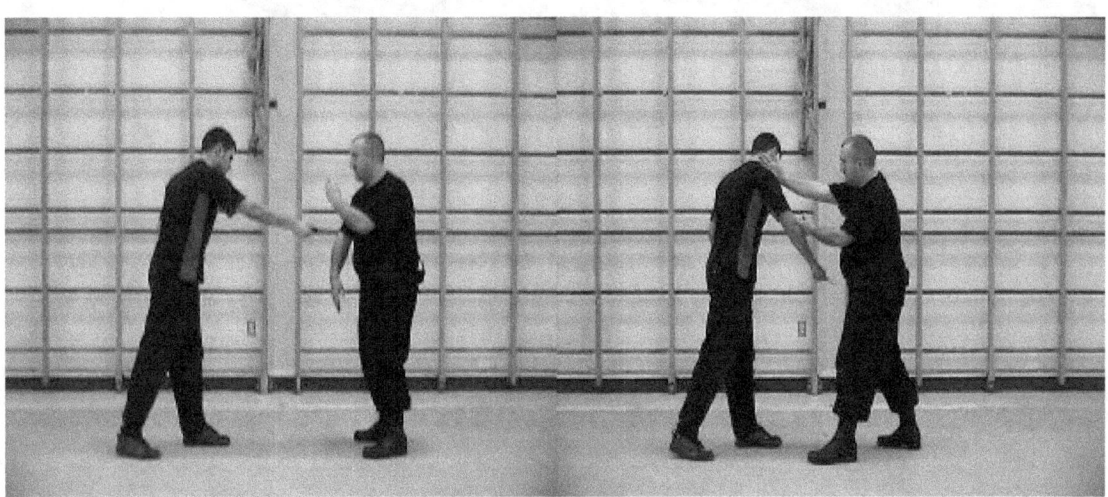

2. Simultaneously strike SI-16 with palm down, rolling it till the thumb hits ST-5 (quadrant 1).

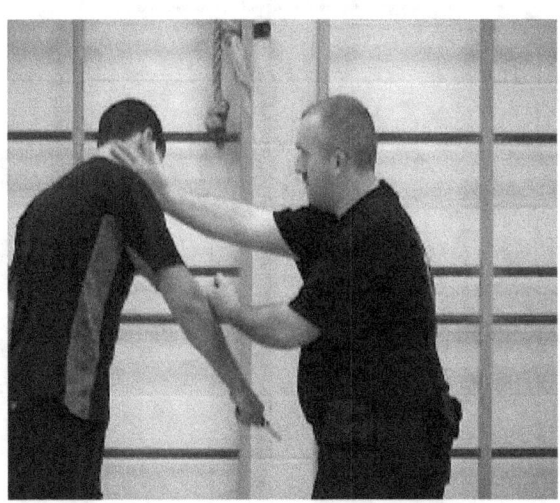

3. Rotate the palm in with thumb down grabbing the left side of his neck at GB-20 (quadrant 2).

MILITARY HAPKIDO: POLICE TACTICAL TRAINING VOL.1

4. Continue the circular motion, shooting your right arm along the opponent's jaw forcing the head to the side and into your armpit while lifting.

5. Apply pressure to LI-17 on the subject's jaw to help maintain control.

6. Take the subject to the ground under control and proceed with appropriate handcuffing techniques.

MILITARY HAPKIDO: POLICE TACTICAL TRAINING VOL.1

CHAPTER FIVE-LESSON SIX
DEFENSE AGAINST A BACKSLASH TO THE LUNGS WITH A SABER GRIP

1. From the outside of the subject's body slap the back of the subject's arm with the fingers extended upward.

2. Simultaneously, with palm down, strike GB-20 (quadrant 1).

3. Proceed with appropriate handcuffing techniques.

MILITARY HAPKIDO: POLICE TACTICAL TRAINING VOL.1

CHAPTER FIVE-LESSON SEVEN
DEFENSE AGAINST A FORWARD SABER SLASH TO THE OTHER LUNG

1. From the inside of the subject's body block with your left hand while striking SI-16 (quadrant 1) with your right hand (a reverse shoto chop). Then roll it till your thumb hits ST-5.

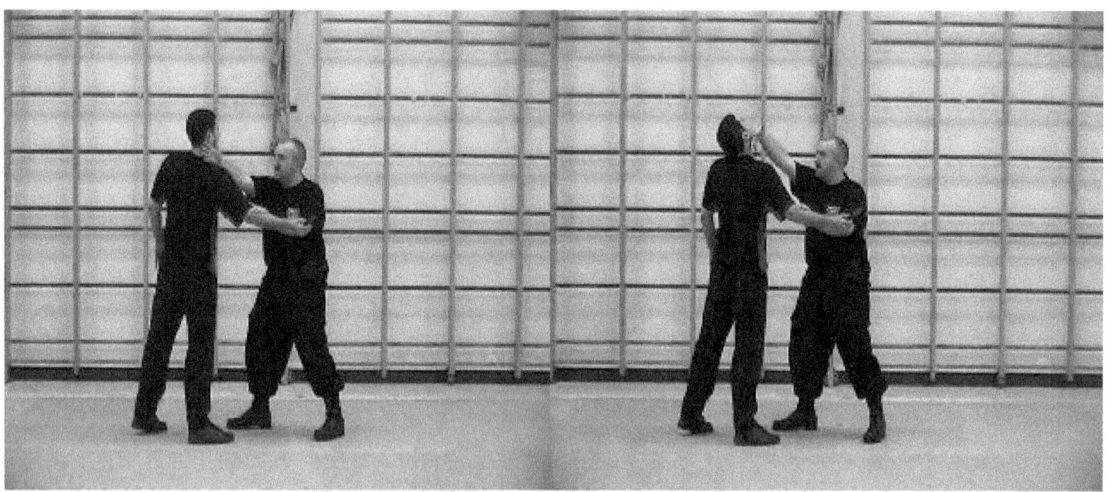

2. Then perform a palm heal strike to CV-24.

MILITARY HAPKIDO: POLICE TACTICAL TRAINING VOL.1

3. Proceed with appropriate handcuffing techniques.

MILITARY HAPKIDO: POLICE TACTICAL TRAINING VOL.1

CHAPTER FIVE-LESSON EIGHT
DEFENSE AGAINST A STRIKE TO THE
CAROTID SINUOUS WITH AN INVERTED REVERSE STAB

1. From the outside of the subject's body strike the subject's arm with your left hand, fingers extended upwards.

2. Simultaneously strike the eyes with your right hand, driving the head back.

MILITARY HAPKIDO: POLICE TACTICAL TRAINING VOL.1

3. Then with your right hand strike CV-24 (chin).

4. Proceed with appropriate handcuffing techniques.

MILITARY HAPKIDO: POLICE TACTICAL TRAINING VOL.1

CHAPTER FIVE-LESSON SEVEN
DEFENSE AGAINST A STRIKE TO THE LEFT CAROTID SINUOUS WITH A FORWARD SLASH

1. Block with your left hand from the inside of the subject's body.

2. Simultaneously with a reverse shoto chop strike SI-16 (quadrant 1) and roll the hand till the thumb strikes ST-5.

3. Rotate the right hand so that the palm is facing inwards and striking GB-20 (quadrant 1).

MILITARY HAPKIDO: POLICE TACTICAL TRAINING VOL.1

4. Grabbing GB-20 (quadrant 2) pull the head downwards.

5. Simultaneously kneeing SP-10 (quadrant 3) with your right knee.

6. Take the subject to the ground under control and proceed with appropriate handcuffing techniques.

MILITARY HAPKIDO: POLICE TACTICAL TRAINING VOL.1

CHAPTER FIVE-LESSON EIGHT
DEFENSE AGAINST A STRIKE WITH A FORWARD SABER SLASH

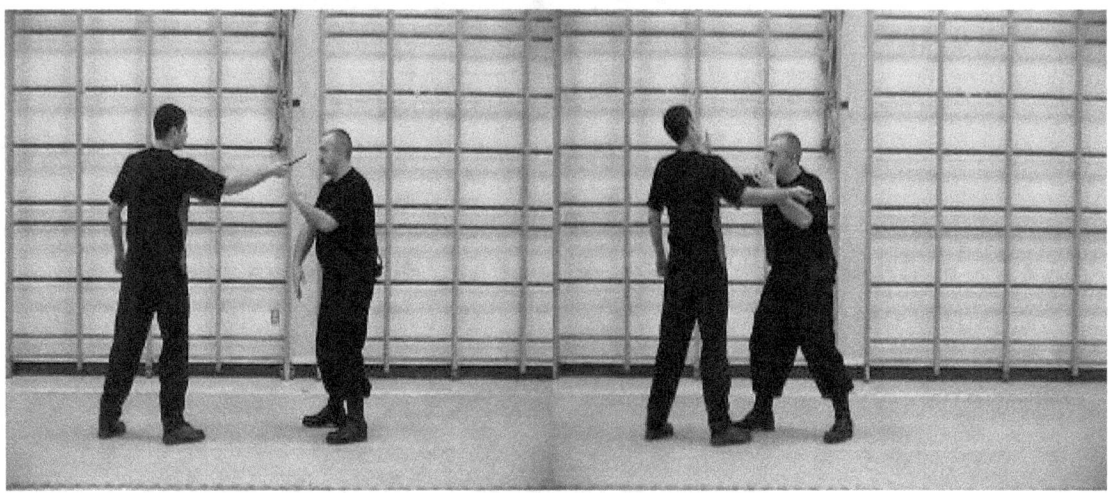

1. Block with your left hand from the inside of the subject's body.

2. Simultaneously striking the left side of the neck to ST-16 (quadrant 2) with palm up and then rolling it into ST-5.

3. As the subject falls to the ground, apply a wrist lock and proceed with appropriate handcuffing techniques.

MILITARY HAPKIDO: POLICE TACTICAL TRAINING VOL.1

CHAPTER VI
HAND GUN DEFENSES

MILITARY HAPKIDO: POLICE TACTICAL TRAINING VOL.1

CHAPTER SIX-LESSON ONE
DEFENSE AGAINST A HANDGUN TO THE FRONT

TECHNIQUE ONE

1. Step to the left and turn clockwise out of the path of the gun. Simultaneously, using your left hand, grasp the subject's right hand with a reverse overhand grab and move it away from you.

2. With your right hand, grasp the barrel of the gun and turn it up and towards the subject, peeling it from the subjects hand (it might be hot if the weapon has already been fired, but remember your life is at stake).

MILITARY HAPKIDO: POLICE TACTICAL TRAINING VOL.1

3. Strike the subject's face with the gun in a forward motion, follow through.

4. Then bring the gun back striking the back of the subject's head.

5. Continue in this motion forcing the subject to roll in a circular motion.

MILITARY HAPKIDO: POLICE TACTICAL TRAINING VOL.1

6. Restrain subject in arm lock with gun cocked and ready to go.

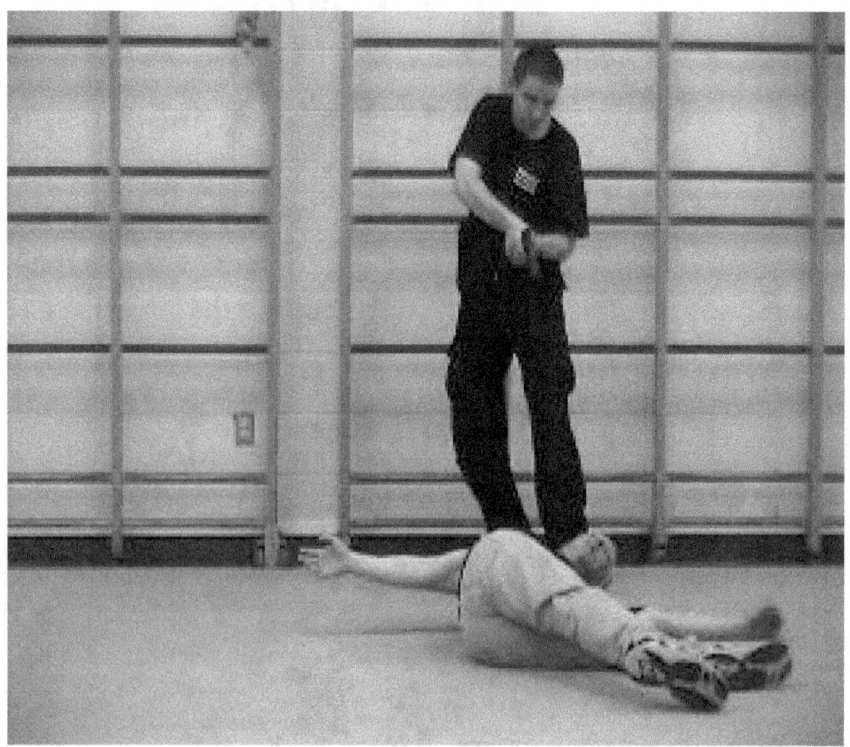

MILITARY HAPKIDO: POLICE TACTICAL TRAINING VOL.1

TECHNIQUE TWO

1. Step to the left and turn clockwise out of the path of the gun. Simultaneously, using both hands, grasp the subject's right hand with a reverse overhand grab and move it away from you.

2. Turn the subject's right hand counterclockwise and in, so that the weapon points straight at the subject.

3. Walk into the subject and continue to turn his right arm so that it goes to the right side of his body over and beyond his elbow.

4. Removing your right hand, peel the gun away from the subject, leaving the follow-up at your command.

MILITARY HAPKIDO: POLICE TACTICAL TRAINING VOL.1

CHAPTER SIX-LESSON TWO
DEFENSE AGAINST A HANDGUN TO THE SIDE

TECHNIQUE ONE

1. Turn counterclockwise and, using your left hand, block and grab the subject's hand using a reverse overhand grab.

2. Simultaneously, using your right hand, strike and grasp the dental pressure points on the subjects face.

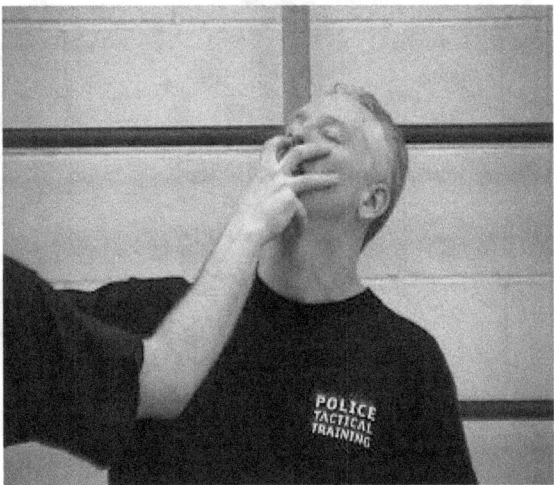

3. Maintaining grasp of the subject's face with your right hand, push the subject's head back and downward, forcing the subject to the ground.

MILITARY HAPKIDO: POLICE TACTICAL TRAINING VOL.1

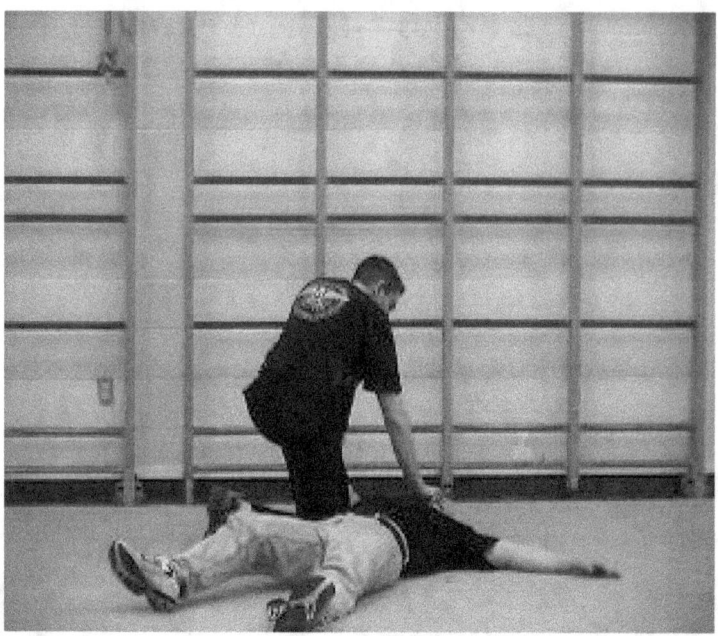

4. Simultaneously, as the subject is taken to the ground, keep your left knee up. Place the subject's gun arm across your knee. Apply downward pressure to the wrist, bending the arm in the wrong direction at the elbow until the subject releases the weapon.

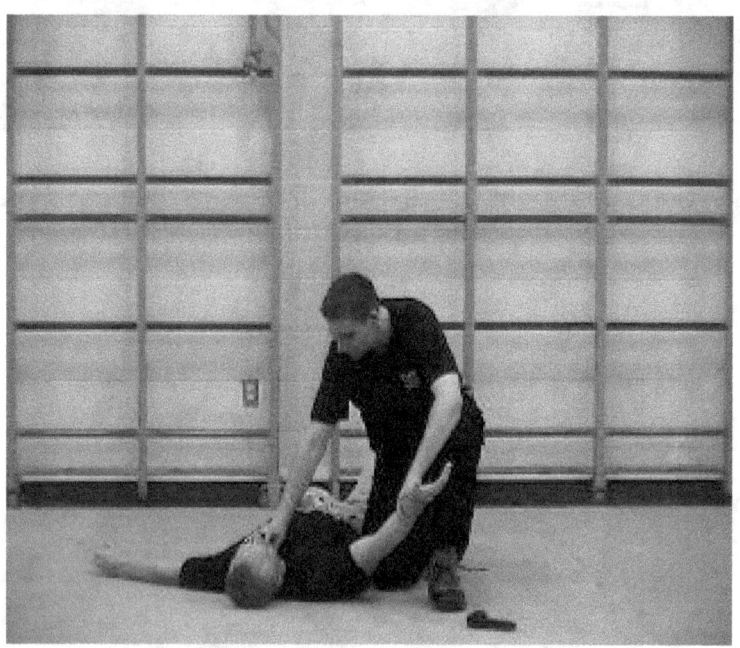

MILITARY HAPKIDO: POLICE TACTICAL TRAINING VOL.1

TECHNIQUE TWO

1. Turn clockwise and, using your right hand, block and grab the subject's hand using a reverse overhand grab.

2. Continue turning clockwise into the subject, extending the subjects arm across your chest. Overextending the subject's are will force the subject to drop the weapon.

MILITARY HAPKIDO: POLICE TACTICAL TRAINING VOL.1

3. Simultaneously, using your left hand apply pressure to the base of the jaw (Small Intestine 17), upward and back. This will force the subject to the ground.

4. As the subject falls, overextend the subject's right arm over your knee as a precaution, in case the weapon is still present. Continue applying pressure until the subject releases the weapon.

MILITARY HAPKIDO: POLICE TACTICAL TRAINING VOL.1

CHAPTER SIX-LESSON THREE
DEFENSE AGAINST A CLOSE HANDGUN TO THE REAR

1. Ensuring your hands are in a "hands up" submissive manner turn clockwise and using your left hand jam the subject's gun into his body. Simultaneously, strike the subject in the groin as a distraction with your right hand to aid in pinning his arm between your body and his.

2. Jamming the gun in closer to the subject's neck reverse your direction throwing the subject over your right leg to the ground.

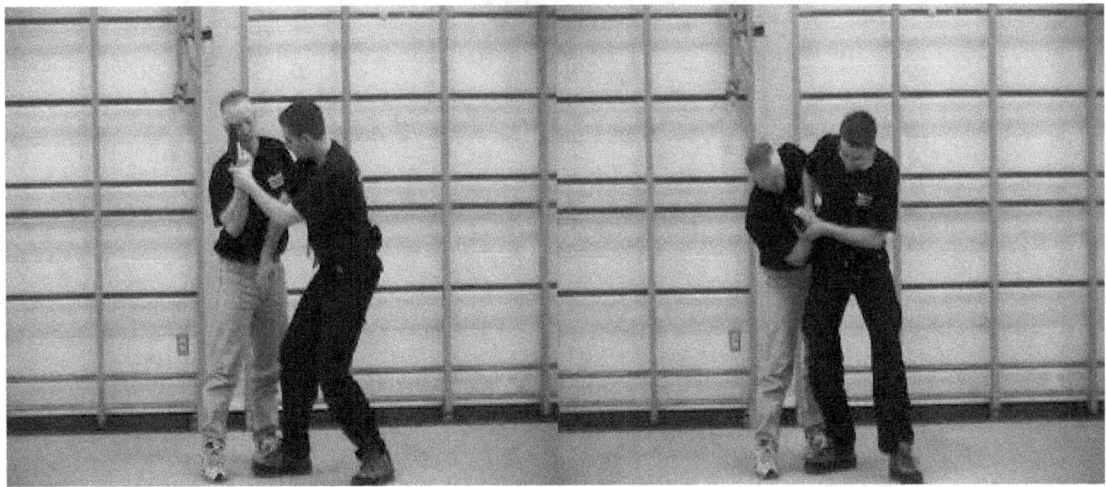

3. As the subject goes to the ground, stay close, maintain the lock on his gun arm and land on him.

MILITARY HAPKIDO: POLICE TACTICAL TRAINING VOL.1

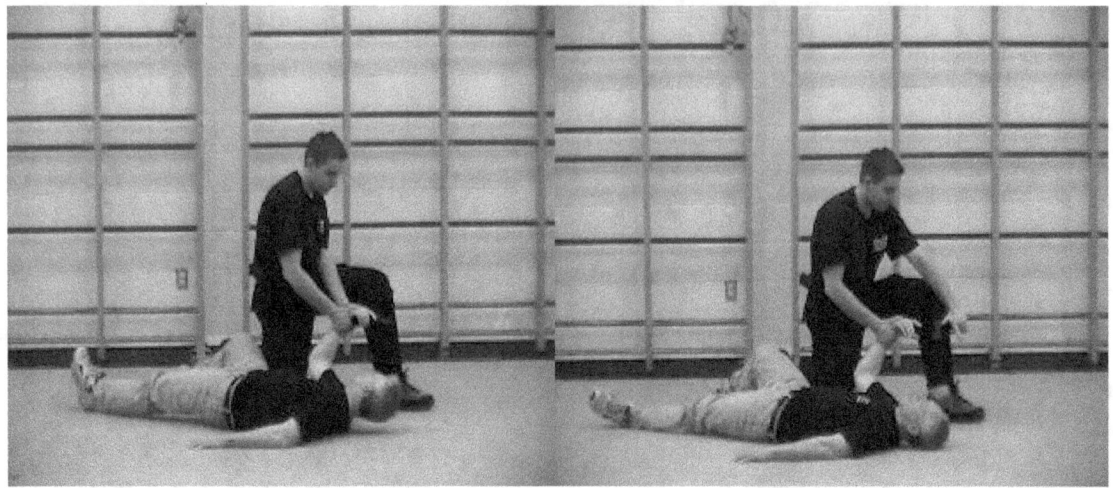

4. On impact remove the gun from the subject's hand and follow-up at your discretion.

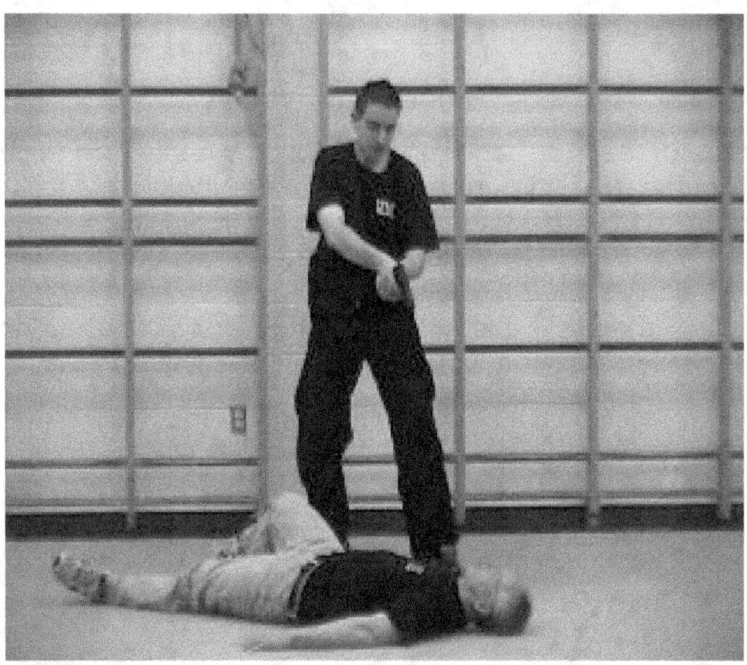

MILITARY HAPKIDO: POLICE TACTICAL TRAINING VOL.1

TECHNIQUE TWO

1. Ensuring your hands are in a "hands up" submissive manner turn counterclockwise into the subject. Using your left arm, clear the gun arm away. Simultaneously, strike the subjects neck with the right hand. Continue to turn, weaving your left arm under the subject's right arm and bringing your right arm over the subject's shoulder.

2. Apply pressure to the subjects head with your left hand, forcing the subject's head to the left and up. Simultaneously, apply pressure to the opposite side of the subject's neck with your right arm to maintain control.

MILITARY HAPKIDO: POLICE TACTICAL TRAINING VOL.1

3. Staying close to the subject so that he cannot move his gun arm, sweep the subject to the ground with your right leg.

4. As the subject goes to the ground, stay close, maintain the lock on his gun arm and land on him.

5. On impact remove the gun from the subject's hand and follow-up at your discretion.

MILITARY HAPKIDO: POLICE TACTICAL TRAINING VOL.1

CHAPTER VII
FORCE CONCEPTS

MILITARY HAPKIDO: POLICE TACTICAL TRAINING VOL.1

SAMPLE FORCE CONTINUUM

SUBJECT ACTION	DEFENDER RESPONSE
Cooperation	Verbal Commands
Passive Resistance	Escort Control
Active Resistance	Control & Compliance Holds
Assault Which Can Result in Bodily Harm	Defensive Tactics/Mechanical Controls/Less Lethal Weapons
Assault Which Can Result In Serious Bodily Harm or Death	Deadly Force

*The use of force continuum presented is a general model based on common U.S. use of force guidelines. The continuum presented is for illustrative purposes only. Any other person utilizing Military Hapkido is responsible for following all applicable local, state or federal laws.

MILITARY HAPKIDO: POLICE TACTICAL TRAINING VOL.1

FORCE CONTINUUM

The force continuum is a conceptual tool which exists to aid Defenders in determining what level of force is required and justified in controlling the actions of an assailant. Verbal commands, escort techniques, mechanical controls, and deadly force are all options which are available to a Defender depending upon the assailants actions. Force escalation must cease when the assailant complies with the commands of the Defender, and/or the situation is controlled by the Defender. The model presented bellow consists of five levels. Physical defensive tactics are appropriate from levels three to five.

Level One: The assailant cooperates with the Defender's verbal commands. Physical actions is not required.

Level Two: The assailant is unresponsive to verbal commands. Assailant cooperation however is achieved with escort techniques.

Level Three: The assailant actively resists the Defender's attempts to control without being assault. Compliance and control holds as well as pain compliance techniques are appropriate actions at this time.

Level Four: The assailant assaults a Defender or another person with actions which are likely to cause bodily harm. Appropriate action would include mechanical controls or defensive tactics such as stunning techniques. Impact and chemical weapons may be appropriate at this level.

Level Five: The assailant assaults a Defender or another person with actions which are likely to cause serious bodily harm or death if not stopped immediately. Appropriate Defender action would include deadly force through mechanical controls, Impact weapons or firearms. Deadly force should be considered only when lesser means have been exhausted, are unavailable or cannot be reasonably employed.

At all levels of the force continuum Defenders must follow the use of force guidelines, policy, and general orders of their employing agency as well as any local, state or federal laws which supersedes any recommendations made by the Military Hapkido staff or program.

DECISION OF FORCE

When making the decision to use force a Defender should use the minimal amount of "Reasonable" force necessary to safely control the situation at hand. When using a blade for self defense a Defender must be prepared to articulate and justify their use of a deadly weapon. By definition a blade should not be employed unless the Defender has deemed the situation at hand to be a lethal force conflict devoid of reasonable access to escape.

"Reasonable force" can be defined: *force that is not excessive and is the least amount of force that will permit safe control of the situation while still maintaining a level of safety for himself or herself and the public.*

A Defender is justified in the use of force when they reasonably believe it to be necessary to defend themselves or another from bodily harm and have no avenue for reasonable escape.

Escalation and de-escalation of resistance and response may occur without going through each successive level. The Defender has the option to escalate or disengage, repeat the technique, or escalate to any level at any time. However, the Defender will need to justify any response to resistance. If the Defender skips levels, he or she must explain why it was necessary to do so.

TOTALITY OF CIRCUMSTANCES

Totality of circumstances refers to all facts and circumstances known to the Defender at the time. The totality of circumstances includes consideration of the assailant's form of resistance, all reasonably perceived factors that may have an effect on the situation, and the response options available to the Defender.

MILITARY HAPKIDO: POLICE TACTICAL TRAINING VOL.1

SAMPLE FACTORS MAY INCLUDE THE FOLLOWING:

- Severity of the assault or battery
- Assailant is an immediate threat
- Assailant's mental or psychiatric history, if known to the Defender
- Assailant's violent history, if known to the Defender
- Assailant's combative skills
- Assailant's access to weapons
- Innocent bystanders who could be harmed
- Number of assailant's vs. number of Defenders
- Duration of confrontation
- Assailant's size, age, weight, and physical condition
- The Defender's size, age, weight, physical condition, and defensive tactics expertise
- Environmental factors, such as physical terrain, weather conditions, etc.

In all cases where your assessment and decision are questioned you may need to demonstrate the following:

- That you felt physically threatened by and in danger from the suspect, i.e. that the suspect's behavior (body language/ words / actions) were aggressive and threatening;

- That you used force as a last resort, and that you used the reasonable amount;

- That you stopped using force once you had the suspect and the situation under control.

- That the Defender has exhausted all reasonable efforts to escape the situation.

MILITARY HAPKIDO: POLICE TACTICAL TRAINING VOL.1

CHAPTER VIII
PRESSURE POINTS

MILITARY HAPKIDO: POLICE TACTICAL TRAINING VOL.1

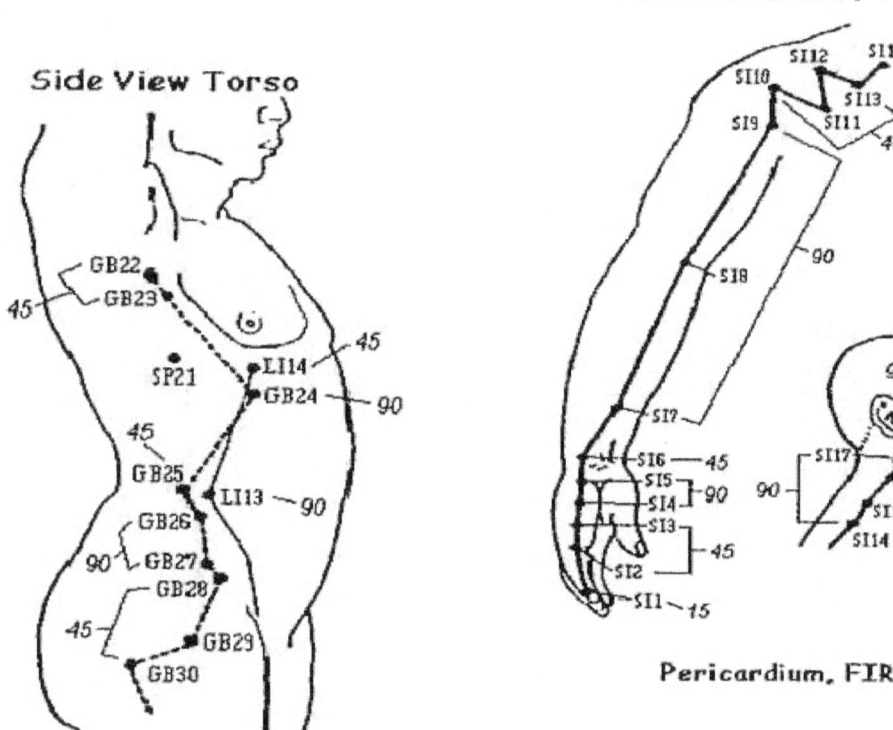

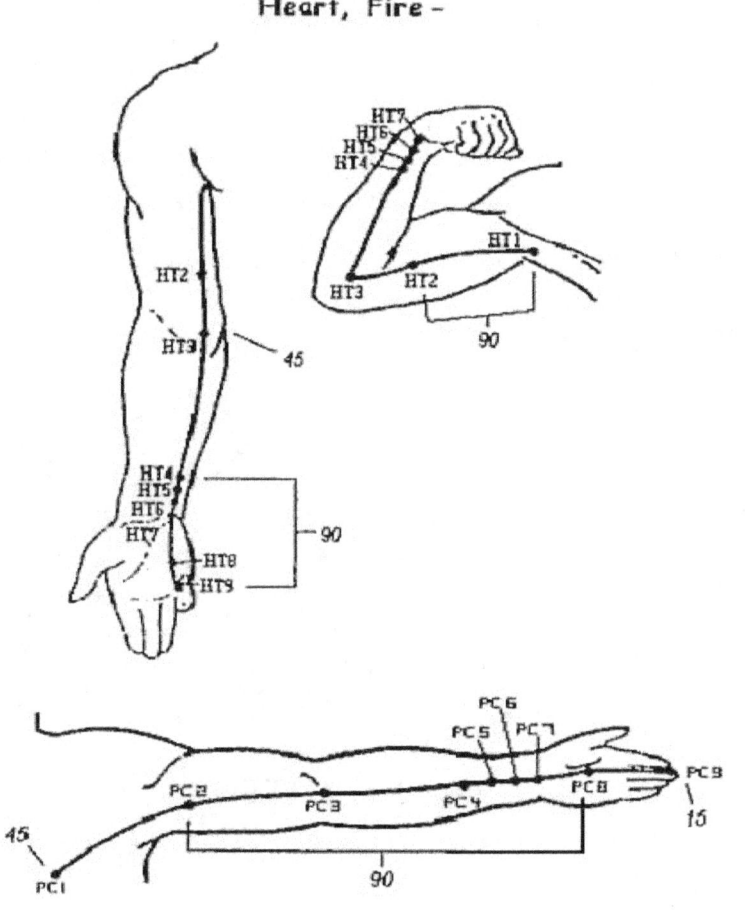

MILITARY HAPKIDO: POLICE TACTICAL TRAINING VOL.1

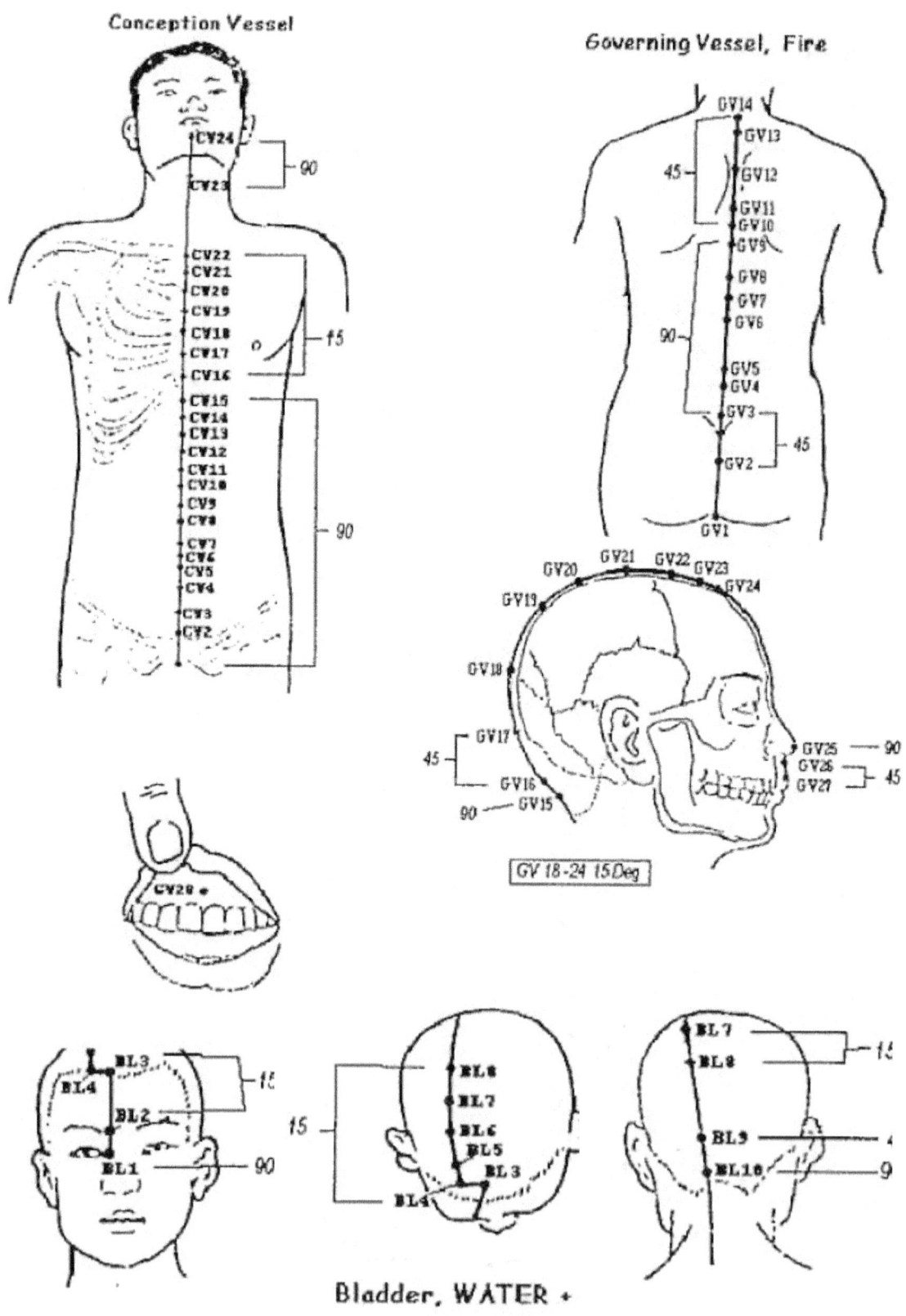

MILITARY HAPKIDO: POLICE TACTICAL TRAINING VOL.1

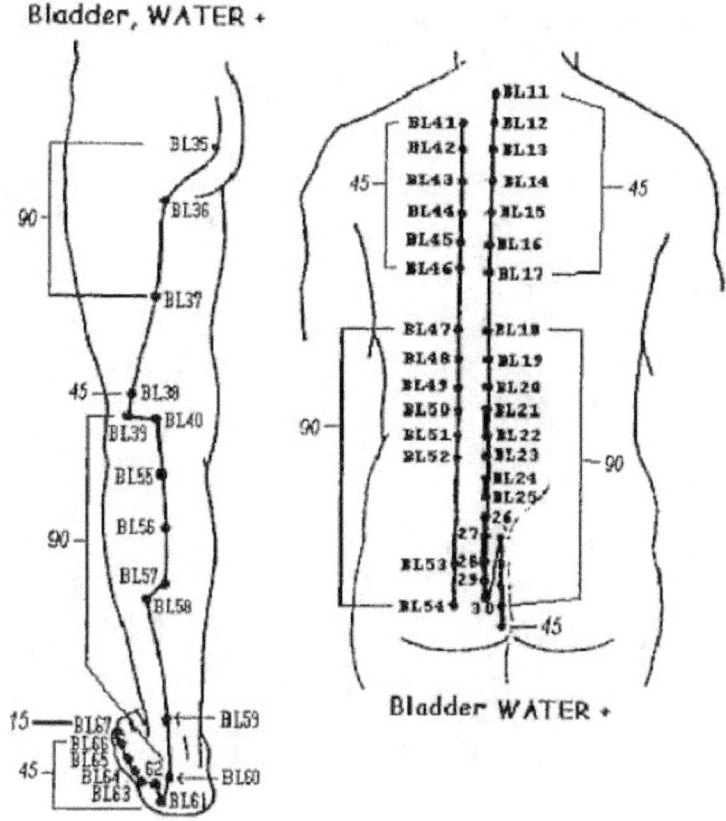

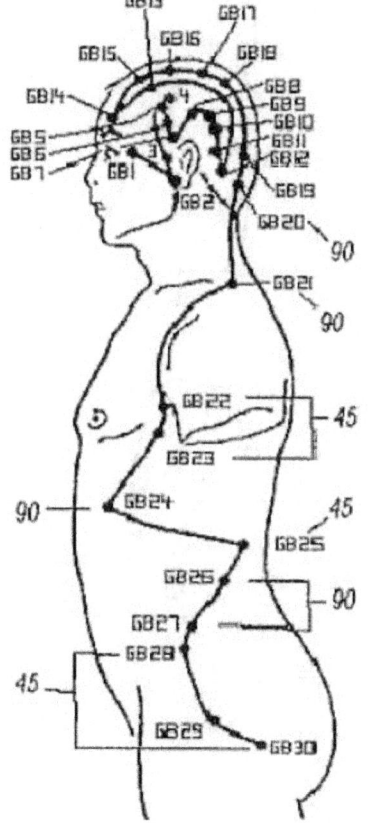

MILITARY HAPKIDO: POLICE TACTICAL TRAINING VOL.1

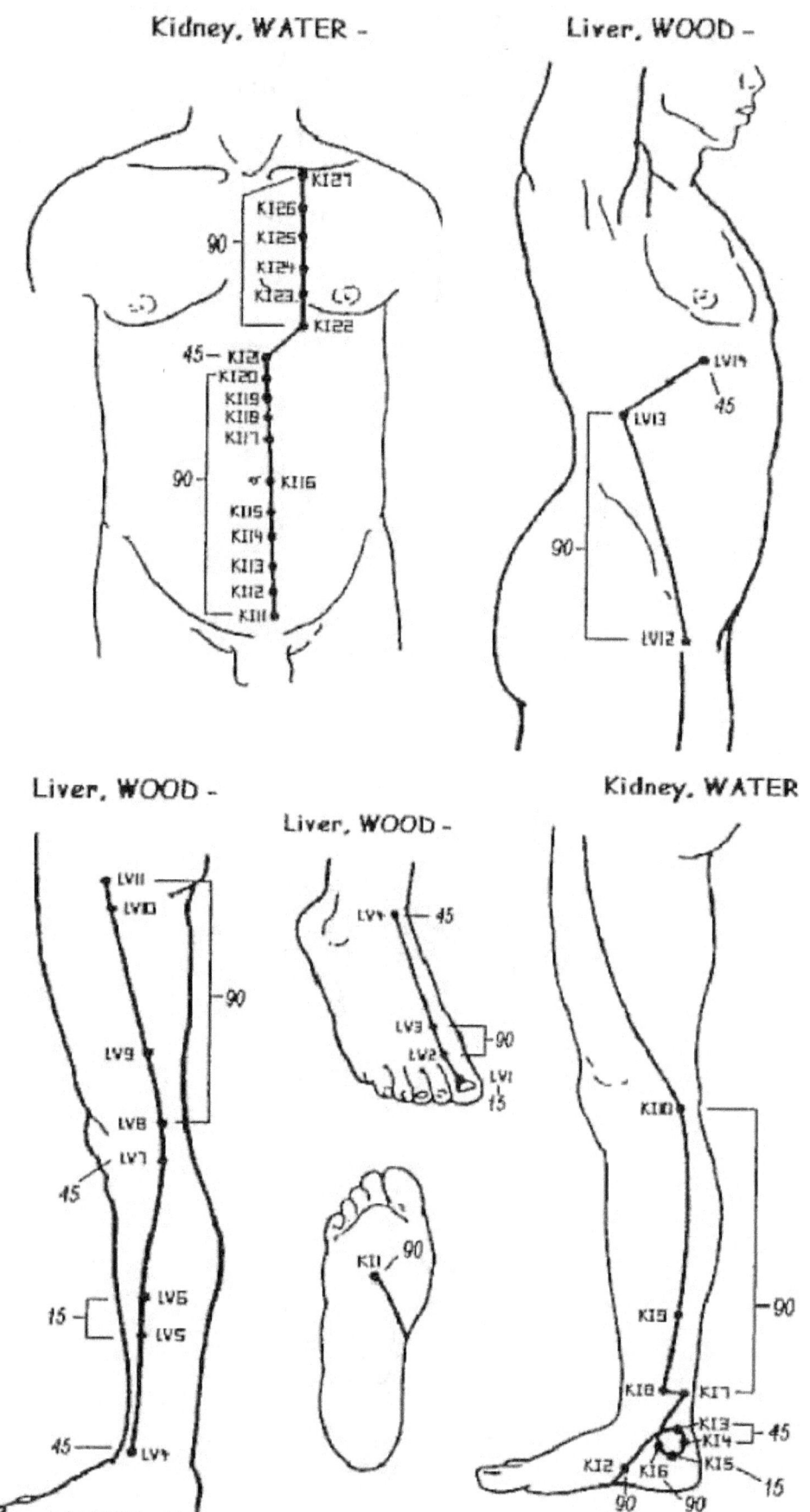

MILITARY HAPKIDO: POLICE TACTICAL TRAINING VOL.1

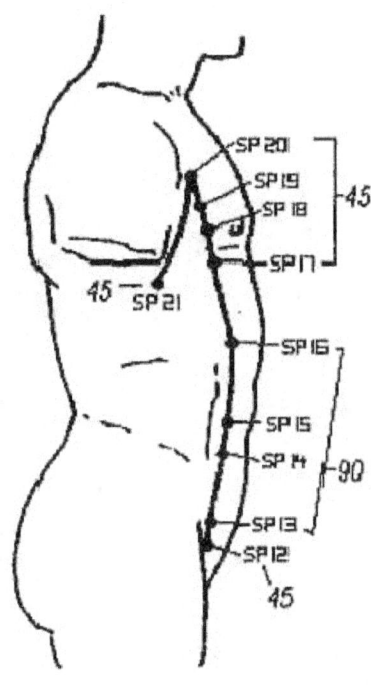

Spleen, EARTH −

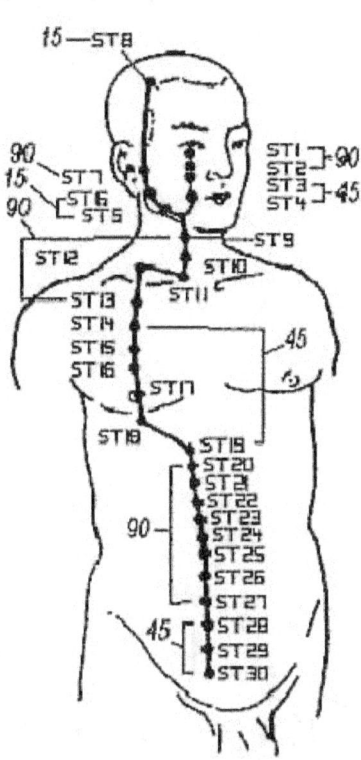

Stomach, EARTH +

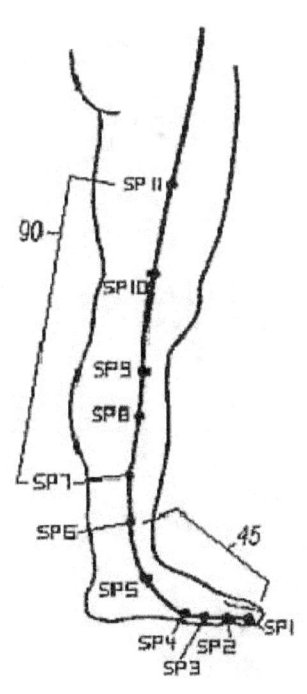

Spleen, EARTH +

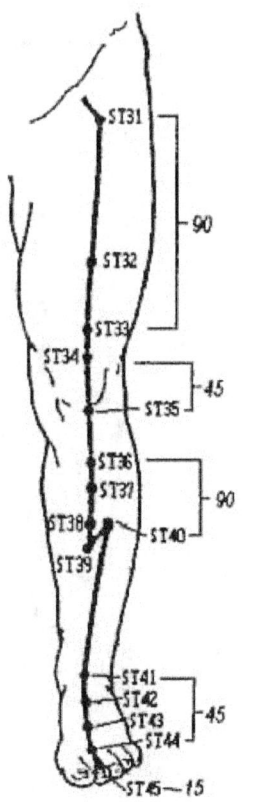

Stomach, Earth +

MILITARY HAPKIDO: POLICE TACTICAL TRAINING VOL.1

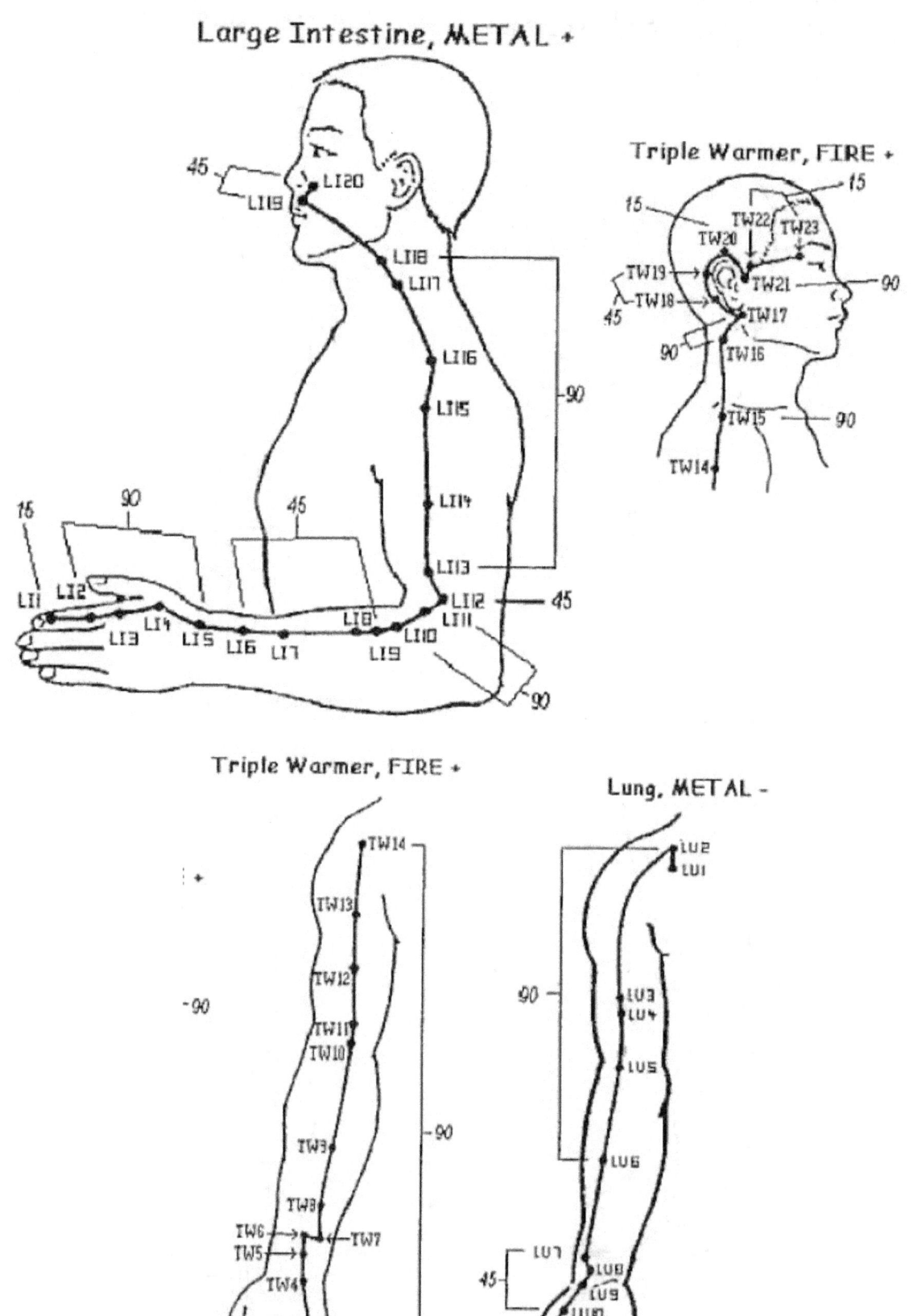

MILITARY HAPKIDO: POLICE TACTICAL TRAINING VOL.1

ADDITIONAL INFORMATION

MILITARY HAPKIDO: POLICE TACTICAL TRAINING VOL.1

RANK TESTING INFORMATION

There are a number of schools in the United States and Canada that are affiliated with Military Hapkido International as well as independent instructors who are qualified to issue rank in the Military Hapkido System. Membership to the association is available to all legitimate students and instructors looking to cross over to the Military Hapkido Systems

Non-traditional testing is available for those who do not live near a qualified instructor. A student who has a suitable understanding/experience and has access to the Military Hapkido manuals and DVDs may be permitted to test for rank via special arrangement with instructors, at Military Hapkido seminars, or via interview and video testing (via youtube, skype, etc).

While non-traditional learning and testing methods are available for those who are unable to attend formal classes, it should be mentioned that we still consider in-person instruction with live feedback from a qualified teacher to be the best method of learning.

For more information about joining Military Hapkido International and The Black Arts Military Unarmed Combat Federation direct all inquiries to:

www.MilitaryHapkido.com
&
www.Black-arts-society.com

Seminars and instructional video tapes can be ordered at the above addresses.

LEFT BLANK INTENTIONALLY

www.ingramcontent.com/pod-product-compliance
Lightning Source LLC
Chambersburg PA
CBHW080931170526
45158CB00008B/2250